EYE ON
Art

FRANK LLOYD WRIGHT

by Don Nardo

LUCENT BOOKS
A part of Gale, Cengage Learning

GALE
CENGAGE Learning·

Detroit • New York • San Francisco • New Haven, Conn • Waterville, Maine • London

GALE
CENGAGE Learning™

LIBRARY OF CONGRESS CATALOGING-IN-PUBLICATION DATA

Nardo, Don, 1947-
  Frank Lloyd Wright / by Don Nardo.
    p. cm. -- (Eye on art)
  Summary: "These books provide a historical overview of the development of different types of art and artistic movements; explore the roots and influences of the genre; discuss the pioneers of the art and consider the changes the genre has undergone"-- Provided by publisher.
  Includes bibliographical references and index.
  ISBN 978-1-4205-0813-0 (hardback)
  1. Wright, Frank Lloyd, 1867-1959--Juvenile literature. 2. Architects--United States--Biography--Juvenile literature. I. Title.
  NA737.W7N37 2012
  720.92--dc23
  [B]
                                                        2012002242

Lucent Books
27500 Drake Rd
Farmington Hills MI 48331

ISBN-13: 978-1-4205-0813-0
ISBN-10: 1-4205-0813-X

CONTENTS

Foreword

"Art has no other purpose than to brush aside . . . everything that veils reality from us in order to bring us face to face with reality itself."

—French philosopher Henri-Louis Bergson

Some thirty-one thousand years ago, early humans painted strikingly sophisticated images of horses, bison, rhinoceroses, bears, and other animals on the walls of a cave in southern France. The meaning of these elaborate pictures is unknown, although some experts speculate that they held ceremonial significance. Regardless of their intended purpose, the Chauvet-Pont-d'Arc cave paintings represent some of the first known expressions of the artistic impulse.

From the Paleolithic era to the present day, human beings have continued to create works of visual art. Artists have developed painting, drawing, sculpture, engraving, and many other techniques to produce visual representations of landscapes, the human form, religious and historical events, and countless other subjects. The artistic impulse also finds expression in glass, jewelry, and new forms inspired by new technology. Indeed, judging by humanity's prolific artistic output throughout history, one must conclude that the compulsion to produce art is an inherent aspect of being human, and the results are among humanity's greatest cultural achievements: masterpieces such as the architectural marvels of ancient Greece, Michelangelo's perfectly rendered statue *David*, Vincent van Gogh's visionary painting *Starry Night*, and endless other treasures.

The creative impulse serves many purposes for society. At its most basic level, art is a form of entertainment or the means for a satisfying or pleasant aesthetic experience. But art's true power lies not in its potential to entertain and delight but in its ability to enlighten, to reveal the truth, and by doing so to uplift the human spirit and transform the human race.

One of the primary functions of art has been to serve religion. For most of Western history, for example, artists were paid by the church to produce works with religious themes and subjects. Art was thus a tool to help human beings transcend mundane, secular reality and achieve spiritual enlightenment. One of the best-known, and largest-scale, examples of Christian religious art is the Sistine Chapel in the Vatican in Rome. In 1508 Pope Julius II commissioned Italian Renaissance artist Michelangelo to paint the chapel's vaulted ceiling, an area of 640 square yards (535 sq. m). Michelangelo spent four years on scaffolding, his neck craned, creating a panoramic fresco of some three hundred human figures. His paintings depict Old Testament prophets and heroes, sibyls of Greek mythology, and nine scenes from the Book of Genesis, including the Creation of Adam, the Fall of Adam and Eve from the Garden of Eden, and the Flood. The ceiling of the Sistine Chapel is considered one of the greatest works of Western art and has inspired the awe of countless Christian pilgrims and other religious seekers. As eighteenth-century German poet and author Johann Wolfgang von Goethe wrote, "Until you have seen this Sistine Chapel, you can have no adequate conception of what man is capable of."

In addition to inspiring religious fervor, art can serve as a force for social change. Artists are among the visionaries of any culture. As such, they often perceive injustice and wrongdoing and confront others by reflecting what they see in their work. One classic example of art as social commentary was created in May 1937, during the brutal Spanish civil war. On May 1 Spanish artist Pablo Picasso learned of the recent attack on the small Basque village of Guernica by German airplanes allied with fascist forces led by Francisco Franco. The German pilots had used the village for target practice, a three-hour bombing that killed sixteen hundred civilians. Picasso, living in Paris, channeled his outrage over the massacre into his painting *Guernica*, a black, white, and gray mural that depicts dismembered animals and fractured human figures whose faces are contorted in agonized expressions. Initially, critics and the public condemned the painting as an incoherent hodgepodge, but the work soon came to be seen as a powerful antiwar statement and remains an iconic symbol of the violence and terror that dominated world events during the remainder of the twentieth century.

The impulse to create art—whether painting animals with crude pigments on a cave wall, sculpting a human form from marble, or commemorating human tragedy in a mural—thus serves many purposes. It offers an entertaining diversion, nourishes the imagination and the spirit, decorates and beautifies the world, and chronicles the age. But underlying all these functions is the desire to reveal that which is obscure—to illuminate, clarify, and perhaps ennoble. As Picasso himself stated, "The purpose of art is washing the dust of daily life off our souls."

The Eye on Art series is intended to assist readers in understanding the various roles of art in society. Each volume offers an in-depth exploration of a major artistic movement, medium, figure, or profession. All books in the series are beautifully illustrated with full-color photographs and diagrams. Riveting narrative, clear technical explanation, informative sidebars, fully documented quotes, a bibliography, and a thorough index all provide excellent starting points for research and discussion. With these features, the Eye on Art series is a useful introduction to the world of art—a world that can offer both insight and inspiration.

Introduction

The Arrogance of the Brilliant

Frank Lloyd Wright is widely viewed as one of the most innovative architects of the late 1800s and early 1900s. But some organizations and authorities have gone much further in their praise. In 1938 *Time* magazine, which put him on its January 17 cover, called him the greatest architect of the twentieth century. Later, in 1991, as part of a retrospective of the art of architecture, the highly prestigious American Institute of Architects (AIA) chose Wright as the "greatest American Architect of all time."[1]

An Astounding Total Output

Whatever Wright's ranking among his colleagues may have been, there can be no doubt that he made an immense and lasting impression on the architectural landscape in the United States, as well as a lesser but still important impact across the globe. His longevity and total output alone verge on the astounding. Wright had a career lasting some seventy years, longer than most people's entire lifetimes. During those years, which were frequently personally turbulent and/or tragic as well as busy for him, he created more than a thousand designs for houses and other buildings. A bit more than half of these were actually built, an unusually large number of finished structures for any architect. Moreover, Wright designed edifices that have stood the test of time, both in their physical integrity and their notoriety. Although a majority of his buildings were erected in the late 1800s and early 1900s, close to 80 percent of them are still standing, and many are viewed as national historic sites and landmarks.

Wright was not famous and respected simply because he was extraordinarily productive, however. His importance as an architect rests mainly on his introduction or widespread popularization of concepts that were later adopted by many other

Frank Lloyd Wright (1869–1959) is considered to be the greatest American architect of all time.

architects and builders. Among others, these included organic architecture (making a structure seem to grow naturally from its surroundings); open floor plans, which subsequently became a common feature of most modern homes; coordinated design elements (making all sections and aspects of a building part of a harmonious whole); using innovative methods for lighting the interiors of buildings; and contributing custom-designed furniture and other furnishings to each project.

In addition to the fame he garnered from his work, Wright was frequently in the news because of his highly unconventional lifestyle and the events of his personal life. The latter ranged from quirky to scandalous to heartbreaking. He was well known as a larger-than-life character. Extremely self-confident, opinionated, and outspoken, he attracted a number of like-minded individuals, many of them apprentice architects, into a sort of communal living and working situation. Art historian Franklin Toker describes this singular arrangement, which came to be called the Taliesin (tah-lee-EH-sin) Fellowship after the name of Wright's beloved home in Spring Green, Wisconsin.

> Wright charged a dozen young architects $675 a year . . . to work with him at Taliesin. That was high tuition in those days, more than live-in students paid at either Harvard or Yale. The young men and women who responded to Wright's offer agreed to plant the crops, tend the livestock, cook and bake their meals, wash their laundry (Wright's too), and hew wood to heat the place. Those who could were expected to play Bach and Beethoven on Saturday nights.[2]

"I Was Under Oath"

The members of the fellowship tended to worship Wright as a kind of professional guru and personal mentor. They were not turned off by his air of supreme self-confidence and authority, which many other people interpreted as arrogance and pomposity. In fact, he acquired a reputation for conceit and haughtiness that he was never able to shake.

Part of Wright's supposed arrogance undoubtedly derived from the manner in which he spoke about his profession. He often elevated it beyond all others, which gave him an aura of self-importance in some people's eyes. "The mother art is architecture," he frequently repeated in the numerous essays, articles, and books he turned out over the years. "Without an architecture of our own we have no soul of our own civilization."[3]

There were also a number of times when Wright's use of certain ill-chosen words further inflated his reputation for personal egotism. One famous episode took place in court, where he appeared as a witness. When he was asked his occupation, he replied that he was "the world's greatest architect." Afterward, his third wife, Olgivanna, scolded him, saying that he had come across as terribly conceited. In classic Wright fashion, he told her, "I had no choice, Olgivanna. I was under oath."[4]

Another public appearance that added fuel to the fire, so to speak, occurred in 1957, when legendary CBS newsman Mike Wallace interviewed Wright, then eighty-eight, on television. Wallace said, "You said many years ago that you would some day be the greatest architect of the twentieth century. Have you reached your goal?" To that, Wright protested, "Well, now I think I never said it." The conversation continued:

WALLACE: Over the years, you have said it not once, but many times. Maybe not . . . in that specific form.

WRIGHT: You know, I may not have said it, but I may have felt it.

WALLACE: Uh-huh. You do feel it?

WRIGHT: But it is so unbecoming to say it that I should have been careful about it. I'm not as crude as I am generally reported to be. I believe, like this matter of arrogance. Now what is arrogance?

WALLACE: What is arrogance?

WRIGHT: Arrogance is something a man possesses on the surface to defend the fact that he hasn't got the thing that he pretends to have. . . .

WALLACE: Arrogance can sometimes be a shell to protect the inner man too, can it not, even though that inner man has a good deal?

WRIGHT: Well, it's a pretty brittle shell. . . . [At any rate] I think that any man who really has faith in himself will be dubbed arrogant by his fellows. I think that's what happened to me. . . . I respect any man or woman who respects himself sufficiently to tell the truth no matter what or who it might hurt.[5]

Monuments for All of Us

Despite claiming to Wallace that he was not arrogant but rather very self-confident and a truth-teller, Wright did admit to being conceited from time to time. Yet he always remained unapologetic for it. "Early in my career," he declared in his later years, "I was a very arrogant young man. I was so sure of my[self] and I had to choose between an honest arrogance and a hyp[o]critical humility [and] I deliberately choose an honest arrogance, and I've never been sorry."[6]

This so-called "honest arrogance" of Wright's seems to have stemmed from his equally honest belief that he and a few other gifted architects had what amounted to a major mission. This was to lead humanity away from centuries of repetitive, unimaginative, and backward-looking architectural styles and designs. He also told Wallace,

Very few architects in the world know anything about it. I've been accused of saying I was the greatest architect in the world, and if I had said so, I don't think it would be very arrogant because I don't believe there are many [really good architects], if any. For five hundred years what we call architecture has been phony.[7]

Wright elaborated on what he meant by unimaginative and phony architecture in his 1954 essay "The Natural House." The "typical American house" had "no sense of unity at all," he said, "nor any such sense of space as should belong to a free people." Such a home was built "in thoughtless fashion" on any plot a builder could get his hands on, regardless of whether the structure looked appropriate in that spot. So-called "modernistic" houses, he added, "are more boxes than houses." Whether made of "brick or wood or stone, this 'house' was a bedeviled box with a fussy lid; a complex box that had to be cut up by all kinds of holes made in it to let in light and air, with an especially ugly hole to go in and come out of."[8]

Wright clearly believed that he was destined to help his country and humanity as a whole. By adopting his ideas, he seemed to say, they could escape from the architectural prison in which they languished. As documentary filmmaker Ken Burns puts it, "The buildings he left, still among the greatest of all American architecture, bear witness to the originality of a man who thought it his duty to convert all of humanity to his way of designing things."[9]

Even if such a self-imposed goal can be labeled arrogant, as opposed to extremely idealistic and confident, in Wright's case it was a special, ultimately benevolent kind of arrogance. The late journalist and social critic Brendon Gill summed it up well when he said that Wright had an "arrogance to create something which is selfless." After all, the fantastic array of magnificent structures he created "are not *his* monuments. They are monuments for all of us and all of us gain from these monuments in a way that is not that simple act of egotism on the part of a great man."[10] In other words, Wright possessed not the tiresome, unattractive conceit of the mere boaster but rather a much rarer and more forgivable foible that one might call the arrogance of the brilliant.

Journey to Oak Park: 1867–1893

On seeing a house or other building designed by Frank Lloyd Wright, many people are struck by how modern and up-to-date it seems, despite the fact that he died more than half a century ago. Those same people are even more amazed when they discover that Wright was born into what today seems a distant, antique age. He came into the world on June 8, 1867, just two years after the close of the American Civil War. In fact, his original middle name—Lincoln—was intended as a gesture of respect to President Abraham Lincoln, who had been shot and killed on April 15, 1865.

Frank Lincoln Wright's tiny hometown of Richland Center in southern Wisconsin, about 170 miles (274km) northwest of Chicago, had been established only sixteen years before his birth. So his father, William, and mother, Anna Lloyd Wright, formerly Anna Lloyd Jones, were among the community's initial handful of residents. William was a school superintendent as well as a Baptist minister who preached at a small church in Richland Center. Anna, who hailed from an old Welsh farming family, was a teacher. Also educators, her sisters Nell and Jane had recently established the Hillside Home School in their own hometown—nearby Spring Green, Wisconsin.

A Crowded Household

Even before Frank was born, Anna had set her mind on his one day becoming an architect, partly because she greatly admired the look of churches and other large, ornately decorated structures. Another likely factor was that her husband made what she viewed as far too little money to raise a family in the manner she would have liked. In contrast, if her son became an architect, a

Determined that her son become a great architect, Wright's mother, Anna Lloyd Wright, was a major influence on her son's decision to enter the field.

well-paying profession, he and his own future family would not live in poverty. Whatever Anna's reasons for singling out architecture may have been, Frank himself later recalled,

> The boy, she said, was to build beautiful buildings. . . . Fascinated by buildings, she took ten full-page wood engravings of the old English cathedrals from "Old England," a pictorial [magazine] to which [her husband] had subscribed, had them framed . . . and hung them upon the walls of the room that was to be her son's.[11]

Anna apparently believed that if she surrounded the young boy with images of great architecture, he would grow to love them and eventually desire to create new buildings of his own. Considering that the boy did grow up to be an enthusiastic and successful architect, her plan appears to have worked. Another way she encouraged young Frank to enjoy architectural forms was to give him a very special toy when he was seven. It was a set of Froebel blocks, designed by noted German educator Friedrich Froebel (1782–1852), who developed the world's first kindergarten programs. One Wright biographer, Robin L. Sommer, explains that the activity-based Froebel game set

> consisted mainly of simply shaped objects in primary colors—cubes, cylinders, squares, and so forth. The child was encouraged to arrange these shapes into structures in various imaginative ways, and, as an adult, Wright claimed that his career in architecture was deeply influenced by this experience.[12]

At Anna's urgings, Frank's sister Jane, whom everyone called Jennie, played with the Froebel blocks, too. But to her they were no more than interesting toys, whereas Frank became quite infatuated with them. Jennie had been born when Frank was two, and he gained another sister, Margaret Ellen, called Meg-Ellen, soon afterward. That made the household fairly crowded, as William Wright already had three young children from a previous marriage when he wed Frank's mother.

All six children did their best to cope with the growing tensions in the house. No matter what job William tried his hand at, he never made much money, and he and Anna increasingly fought over the difficulties of making ends meet. Frank, who early showed signs of penetrating intelligence and a sensitive temperament, often escaped from the family stresses by spending a lot of time by himself. He especially enjoyed reading, drawing, and collecting rocks.

The Man of the House

The family's troubles came to a head in 1885. The frustrated and unhappy William asked his wife for a divorce. No less miserable than he, she responded by telling him that he might as well pack a bag and leave right away, which he swiftly and silently did. Seventeen-year-old Frank never saw his father again.

In a very real sense, Frank was now the man of the house and saw that it was necessary for him to get a job to help pay the bills. His mother arranged for him to become an assistant to Allan D. Conover, a civil engineer with the University of Wisconsin. Conover was also a draftsman (someone who does drawings of buildings or other objects for a living), so although Frank did mainly office work and errands for Conover, he learned a lot about technical drawing from his boss. Meanwhile, Frank took courses in geometry and drawing at the university in his spare time. The young man also changed his middle name from Lincoln to Lloyd, his mother's maiden name, as a way of disassociating himself from his father, toward whom he was still bitter. From the age of eighteen on, the world knew him as Frank Lloyd Wright.

By this time, Wright had set his sights firmly on becoming an architect, which not surprisingly made his mother very happy. Unlike most other aspiring architects of his and later generations, however, he acquired little in the way of formal training. He took only a few courses in math and engineering at the university and had a tendency to skip class. He also never graduated from any college or university.

Instead, Wright learned by experience. Some of it consisted of working with established engineers and architects and absorbing everything he could from them. He also asked people he

Wright was born into an age when for the first time in human history architects and builders were starting to acquire large-scale mastery of materials such as iron, steel, glass, and reinforced concrete, all of which he used for his structures. One of the first early-modern buildings that used some of these items on a major scale was the Crystal Palace, erected shortly before Wright was born. The structure went up in London's Hyde Park as part of the Great Exhibition of 1851, in a sense the first world's fair. The Crystal Palace was 1,850 feet (560m) long, 110 feet (33m) high, and covered 25 acres (10ha). It was made up almost completely of iron girders and large glass panels, an approach to construction that foreshadowed the great skyscrapers of modern cities. The building also showed the utility of prefabricated materials, which Wright would later employ in many of his designs. The Crystal Palace survived until 1936, when it was destroyed in a fire.

Built as part of London's Great Exhibition of 1851, the Crystal Palace was one of the first buildings in which steel, iron, glass, and reinforced concrete were used.

knew to give him small-scale design projects, which allowed him to put some of what he was learning into practice. When his uncle Jenkin, Anna's brother, decided to build a family chapel in Spring Green, for instance, the young man talked him into letting him design the interior. Also, his aunts Jane and Nell wanted to erect a new building for their Hillside Home School. This became the first complete structure Wright ever designed. The three-story shingled building, featuring dormers and a tall chimney, went up in 1887. (It was torn down in 1950. In 1902 Wright designed a second, larger school building that still stands on the property.)

Chicago's Unprecedented Opportunities

Not long after the new school building was completed, Wright felt the urge to move to Chicago and begin a serious career in architecture. He did not choose Chicago simply because it was the nearest large city. Rather, at that time Chicago was, along with New York City, one of the two principal hubs of large-scale building projects in the United States.

Chicago had the added dimension of being the center of a massive wave of new construction following the recent near total destruction of its downtown area. In 1871 the famous Chicago Fire had devastated large sections of the city. This had created unprecedented opportunities for architects and builders to fill large empty spaces with new and hopefully innovative monumental, or large-scale, buildings.

However, young Wright did not see many of the big structures that had so far been erected as being innovative, at least in their outward appearance. He knew full well that they were state-of-the-art (up to date) in their inner workings, the parts that people could not see. This was due to their having partial or full iron frames. Thanks to the Industrial Revolution, which had begun in the 1700s in Britain and was sweeping through North America during Wright's youth, iron and steel had come of age as building materials. Iron bridges were rising everywhere, and architects and builders were applying iron, along with steel and reinforced concrete, to monumental commercial and public buildings. With iron and steel skeletons, the enormous mass of a building—its load—could be both distributed throughout its structure and well supported. So architects could now make a building almost as gigantic as they liked and much taller than was possible in earlier ages.

Wright viewed this underlying structural aspect of ongoing large-scale design and construction as important and exciting. But he was decidedly less enthusiastic about the exteriors of most of the new buildings. To a large extent these were based

Wright was inspired by noted Chicago architect Louis Sullivan, pictured. Before approaching Sullivan about a job, Wright gained experience working for architect Joseph Silsbee.

on or borrowed heavily from past architectural styles, some dating back to or even before the Renaissance. Wright felt that the design elements of too many structures, from public buildings to private houses, were unoriginal and unimaginative, as were the architects who employed them.

He did recognize a few exceptions to this rule, notably Louis Sullivan (1856–1924) of the major Chicago architectural firm of Adler and Sullivan. In Dankmar Adler, Wright saw a fine engineer who understood the structural elements of buildings well but whose architectural designs were not very original. Sullivan, however, Wright correctly reasoned, was a brilliant designer who consistently attempted to avoid rehashing the past and to find ways of advancing the art of architecture.

Wright was eager to work with and learn from Sullivan but knew he needed to get some more basic, practical experience under his belt before approaching someone of that stature. So the young man first landed an eight-dollar-a-week job as a draftsman for Chicago architect Joseph Silsbee. Wright had met Silsbee back in Spring Green. He was a friend of the Lloyd Jones family.

The Poetry of Architecture

During the year in which he worked for Silsbee, Wright met a young woman named Catherine Tobin, whose family and friends called her Kitty. He later described her in a nutshell, saying, "She walked with a kind of light-hearted gaiety. Mass of red curls . . . blue-eyed, frank, and impulsive."[13] The two soon fell in love and after about a year of dating began talking about marriage.

There was no way, however, that a married couple could live on the money the young man earned working for Silsbee. Wright had received a raise from eight to fifteen dollars a week after a few months with the firm. But it was still not enough. This need to make more money factored into Wright's decision in 1888 to leave Silsbee's employ and apply for his dream job at Adler and Sullivan. By that time the young man had become a first-rate draftsman, and the high quality of his sample sketches was enough to land him the new position, which paid twenty-five dollars per week.

It turned out that Wright could not have joined Adler and Sullivan at a more opportune time. The firm had recently been awarded a huge commission—Chicago's new Auditorium Building complex, which included an office building, a hotel, and a forty-two-hundred-seat auditorium for public events and performances. This only served to confirm that Louis Sullivan was in the forefront of American architecture and that Wright could expect to learn from the best.

In fact, Sullivan, who immediately took a liking to Wright, proved to be one of the major influences on the younger man's early visions of what architecture could and should achieve. Sullivan believed that ornamentation, or decorative elements, were important in making a building look attractive or inviting. But he emphasized that such ornaments must not appear to be artificial additions having little or no relation to the building's function. Rather, their form should follow their function. That is, a structure's ornamentation should look like it is integral to, or a natural outgrowth of, that building and its primary uses. This idea inspired Wright, who later incorporated the "form follows function" architectural concept into his own building designs. The Chicago History Museum recently summed up Sullivan's contributions to architecture, including his mentoring of Wright, saying,

> Louis Sullivan played a critical role in establishing Chicago as a hotbed of innovative American architecture in the late 19th century, altering the course of American architecture in the process. Over just two decades, he designed some of the city's most recognized and influential buildings, pioneering new ways of thinking about formal relationships, aspiring to what he called "the poetry of architecture." His innovation and leadership inspired his most famous student, Frank Lloyd Wright, to later call him the "lieber-meister" ("beloved master"). Since his death in 1924, Sullivan

has been widely recognized as a brilliant designer of architectural ornament and an influential mentor to Frank Lloyd Wright.[14]

During his several conversations with Sullivan about what made for good architecture, Wright explained his own budding architectural philosophy. The most important aspect of it revolved around the idea of so-called organic architecture. A

During the year he spent working for Joseph Silsbee, Wright met and began courting the first of his three wives, Catherine Tobin, pictured.

building, he said, should be as much as humanly possible an extension or outgrowth of the natural surroundings in which it rests, rather than something obviously artificial that has simply been placed there. Wright himself described it this way:

> You must read the book of nature. What we must know in organic architecture is not found in books. It is necessary to have recourse to Nature with a capital N in order to get an education. [It is] necessary to learn from trees, flowers, shells—objects which contain truth of form following function. If we stopped there, then it would be merely imitation. But if we dig deep enough to read the principles upon which these are activated, we arrive at secrets of form related to purpose that would make of the tree a building and of the building a tree.[15]

In the case of most houses, which are not organic, Wright held, they tend to give a natural setting a cluttered look. Or they mar the innate order and beauty of their natural settings in other ways. In contrast, he stated, "A good building makes the landscape more beautiful than it was before that building was built."[16]

The Oak Park House

Wright utilized some of these ideas in the first residential home he ever designed, created for himself and Kitty in 1889. To finance the project, he borrowed five thousand dollars, a very large sum at the time, from Louis Sullivan. The house was (and still is) located at the intersection of Chicago and Forest Avenues in Oak Park, Illinois, it still is a quiet suburb of Chicago. The house's exterior was simple and unpainted, and its combination of brick, white stone, and dark wooden shingles made it blend effortlessly with the lovely wooded setting.

With the new house under construction, Wright and Kitty married in June 1889. The following year, they had their first child—Frank Lloyd Wright Jr., whom people called Lloyd for short. A second son, John, came along in 1892, and a daughter,

LOUIS SULLIVAN'S ARCHITECTURAL IDEALS

Wright's chief early influence in architecture was his mentor at the firm of Adler and Sullivan, Louis Sullivan, who was famous for saying that a building's form should follow its function. In its 2006 retrospective of Sullivan and his work, the Chicago History Museum explained his architectural philosophy, saying in part:

Louis Sullivan is perhaps best known for his talent with ornamentation. His designs are easily recognizable. . . . [He] developed a style of ornamentation that reflected nature through symmetrical use of stylized foliage and weaving geometric forms. . . . Some typical features of his ornament are: bold geometric facades dotted with arched openings; walls with highlighted low-relief sculptural elements of terra cotta; flat rooflines and deep projecting eaves; buildings segregated into distinct zones and separated by vertical bands of decoration; vertical alignment of windows; highly decorated friezes [horizontal decorative bands]; and extensive use of ornamental vines and foliage. American and European architects alike are inspired by his intricate designs, which express the building's structure and ornament as one idea. Sullivan believed that ornamentation was not just an afterthought but was integral to the building's overall design.

Chicago History Museum. "Louis Sullivan at 150: Ornament." www.sullivan150.org/about/ornament.php.

As in his design for the Chicago World's Fair's Transportation Building, pictured, Louis Sullivan's style often incorporated geometric facades, arched openings, and low-relief sculptural elements.

Shown here is
Wright's Oak Park
home and studio
near Chicago. The
architect created his
first residential
design in 1889.

Catherine, in 1894. Their fourth child, David, was born a year later, and Frances, the fifth and final addition to the family, arrived in 1897.

It quickly became clear that the building's original space was not big enough to accommodate so many people. So over time Wright expanded the house, erecting a two-story wing that had a large playroom topped by a high, vaulted ceiling. He also added an office-studio where he did most of his designing. Like many, if not most, architects, he thought of his home not only as a place to live in but also as a space to work in. Architect Thomas A. Heinz, an authority on Wright's structures, explains,

> The integration of home and studio reflected Wright's involvement with the Arts and Crafts philosophy advocated by the English architect William Morris [1834–1896]. . . . [In that philosophy] architecture was meant to be a part of an artist or craftsman's life, to be practiced throughout the week. There was no separation between office and home life. Wright lived architecture twenty-four hours a day. His family and children were frequently present in the drafting room during office hours, and he was often there at weekends and during the evenings.[17]

The family's years in the Oak Park house were mostly happy and memorable. Kitty threw dinner parties, some for friends and others for neighbors and other members of the community who might be prospective clients for her husband. In this way she played a direct, helpful role in increasing the family's fortunes. Meanwhile, the children put on skits and plays, sometimes in full costume, in the playroom, festivities in which their father sometimes gleefully took part. The oldest of the brood, Lloyd, later recalled the house's "double-level rooms of one and two stories, scattered vases filled with leaves and wild flowers, [and] massive fireplaces." There were also swords on the walls, a piano, "a life-sized bust of Beethoven," and the playroom was "strewn with queer dolls, building blocks, funny mechanical toys, [and] animals that moved about and wagged their strange heads."[18]

Moonlighting

Although Wright had received raises over the years and was making a reasonable salary at Adler and Sullivan, he and his family had expensive tastes. There never seemed to be quite

The Great Spirit of Architecture

When asked to define architecture in his own words in 1939, Wright said:

Is it the vast collection of the various buildings which have been built to please the varying taste of the various lords of mankind? I think not. No, I know that architecture is life. Or at least it is life itself taking form and therefore it is the truest record of life as it was lived in the world yesterday, as it is lived today, or ever will be lived. So architecture I know to be a Great Spirit. It can never be something that consists of the buildings which have been built by man on Earth . . . mostly now rubbish heaps or soon to be. . . . Architecture is that great creative living spirit which from generation to generation, from age to age, proceeds, persists, creates, according to the nature of man, and his circumstances as they change. That is really architecture.

Quoted in Bruce B. Pfeiffer. *Frank Lloyd Wright: In the Realm of Ideas.* Carbondale: Southern Illinois University Press, 1988, p. 7.

enough money to maintain the standard of living he desired. So he began moonlighting; that is, designing houses on his own at night, behind his bosses' backs, while still working for the firm in the daytime.

The problem was that the contract Wright had signed with Adler and Sullivan specifically prohibited him from designing buildings without the firm's knowledge and permission. Louis Sullivan, who knew many people in the Chicago region, eventually heard through the grapevine about Wright's bootlegging home-design operation. Furious, Sullivan accused Wright of betrayal and fired him.

At this point Wright had no other choice but to strike out on his own and open his own firm. He rented office space in Chicago's Schiller Building, where he met with prospective clients, while continuing to do most of his designs at home. One day in 1894 a man named William H. Winslow walked into the downtown office and asked whether Wright would be interested in designing a house for him. This marked the start of a legendary solo architectural career that was destined to change the very nature of everyday life in America.

2

Homes in the Prairie: 1894–1910

"I stand before you," Frank Lloyd Wright said toward the end of his life, "preaching organic architecture, declaring organic architecture to be the modern ideal."[19] He uttered words to that effect many times during his long career, including during his early years as an independent architect. This was because the concept of organic architecture, or the creation of buildings that seem to grow out of their surroundings, inspired him early and remained with him always. Over the years he utilized a number of architectural styles that expressed the organic ideal. The most famous of these styles, used chiefly for residential family dwellings, is most often called the Prairie House or Prairie Home style.

Contrary to mistaken claims in some modern articles and books, Wright did not invent the Prairie style. Rather, he developed his own distinctive brand of it and more than anyone else popularized it in the American social consciousness. In the 1890s, during and especially after his break with Adler and Sullivan, Wright came to know and discuss architectural ideas with about twenty other young Chicago-based architects who had in common their admiration for Sullivan and what they viewed as his inspiring designs. The informal group, which included popular early-modern architects Dwight Perkins (1867–1941) and Myron Hunt (1868–1952), has come to be called the "Prairie School." (At the time, however, Wright and the others did not use that term, which was coined by architectural historians in the 1960s, after most in the original group had passed away. Instead, they had used a variety of terms, including "Chicago Group.") The Prairie style developed collectively out of the discussions among the members of the Prairie School.

Wright designed the William H. Winslow House in River Forest, Illinois. After Wright left Adler and Sullivan in 1894, Winslow became his first client.

The house Wright designed in 1894 for William H. Winslow, the first customer who approached him after the split with Adler and Sullivan, was not strictly in the Prairie style. Simple and elegant, it looked a bit like an Italian villa. Yet it bore elements of the Prairie style—including naturally colored flat bricks, horizontal roof and window lines, and a flattened, overhanging roof. Not long afterward, Wright perfected these and other Prairie design features in the first masterpiece of the genre—the Ward W. Willits House (1901). Several more Prairie Homes followed in Wright's busy and fruitful 1894–1910 phase, including the classic Frederick C. Robie House (1910). That phase also included his first commercial building, as well as a church that was strikingly unlike any other built before it.

Battling Reliance on the Past

To grasp how revolutionary these early buildings of Wright's were at the time, it is necessary to understand how their styles developed. For the most part, they were a reaction to, or battle against, traditional American architecture. In the century-and-a-half before and even during Wright's 1894–1910 phase, the vast majority of architects relied heavily on older, often rehashed styles and methods. Their frequent tendency to combine elements from some or all of these past styles came to be called Beaux-Arts architecture. It was not only eclectic but also busy with ornamentation, including detailed sculptures and other carvings, Greek-style columns, marble staircases with elaborate banisters, and other richly layered details.

In these ways, "architecture in America took refuge in the past," Franklin Toker explains. In the late 1800s and early 1900s, he writes, all but a handful of American architects were not progressives like Wright, but conservatives who fell back on tradition. Typically, they

> wrapped their steel skeletons in the historicist dress of the Classical [Greco-Roman], Gothic, Renaissance, Baroque, or Georgian styles. Conservative architects [dominated] the [architectural] profession in the

United States from the 1893 World's Fair in Chicago right through the early 1950s. The huge new buildings created for Franklin Roosevelt's Depression-era Washington, D.C., in the 1930s showed how much power the conservatives still had. . . . The new Supreme Court [building erected in] 1935 presented itself as a Greek temple of such unabashed classicism that except for its electrical wiring it could have carried the date of 1835 or [even] 435 B.C.[20]

This reliance on older styles irked Wright to no end during his 1894–1910 phase. He later expressed his regret that at the time most Americans were

almost completely ignorant of our own architecture, or, for that matter, of any architecture except that taught by the Paris Beaux-Arts [schools] or [the] old "Colonial" [style]. Old Colonial derived by the English from France and by France from medieval Italy. Italy was indebted to Greece, Greece to Egypt, and Egypt to—? . . . American society, worldly-rich, was utterly poor in art and afraid to live as itself. Fearful of being ridiculed for lacking knowledge of art, we felt much safer in buying "culture" ready-made from abroad.[21]

Wright was concerned not only about the grip of conservative architects on the growing market for skyscrapers, banks, department stores, and other large public buildings. He saw that the conservatives also dominated the market for smaller-scale house designs, where his main personal interest as an architect lay. This was always a potential impediment to the success of his new firm. Indeed, as Toker points out, "So secure was traditionalism" in architecture that in the early 1900s some towns "prohibited the construction of homes in the modern style, and banks were notorious in refusing to finance them."[22]

Beyond the mere financial and business aspects of designing his Prairie houses, Wright felt that he had a sort of calling to oppose and help to change the conservative, unoriginal approach to architecture then in vogue. He dreamed of a newer, more original American style of architecture. "Conceive that there" might appear "a new sense of building on American soil," he later recalled. That fresh approach, he said,

> could *grow* building forms not only true to function but expressive far beyond mere function, in the realm of the human spirit. Our new country might now have a true architecture hitherto [before now] unknown. Yes, architecture might extend the bounds of human individuality indefinitely by way of interior discipline. Not only [would] space come on a new technique of its own, but every material and every method might now speak for itself in objective terms of human life.[23]

A Model for the Future

In the decade or so following the establishment of his own firm, Wright addressed this need for a distinctly American form of architecture by developing a general design policy. As might be expected, it incorporated his growing list of ideas about organic architecture, in which a building grows out of and blends with its natural surroundings. First, he said, there should be only as many rooms in the house as the occupants actually need and will use on a regular basis. Second, openings such as windows and doors should not be placed randomly, but in ways that are both useful for the particular situation and pleasing to the eye. Third, fixtures, furniture, and other furnishings should complement the design and become a part of the house's basic fabric. In addition, Wright wrote,

> we should recognize and accentuate this natural beauty [using] gently sloping roofs, low proportions, quiet skylines, suppressed heavyset chimneys, sheltering overhangs, low terraces, and outreaching walls [incorporating] private gardens. . . . Go to the woods and fields for color schemes. Use the soft, warm optimistic tones of earths and autumn leaves, [as] they are more wholesome and better adapted in most cases to good decoration.[24]

FURNISHINGS ALSO
PART OF THE HOUSE

Wright felt that a house needed to be more than its floor-plan, walls, and roof. To be truly organic, as well as stylistically well integrated, with all elements complementing or matching one another, the furnishings within the structure should be part of the overall initial plan envisioned by the architect. That way, the entire building, including everything in it, is, in a sense, a single object. In 1910 he said:

In organic architecture . . . it is quite possible to consider the building as one thing, its furnishings another, and its setting and environment still another. [But] the spirit in which these buildings are conceived sees all these together at work as one thing. All are to be studiously foreseen and provided for in the nature of the structure. All these should become mere details of the character and completeness of the structure. Incorporated [are] lighting, heating, and ventilation. The very chairs and tables, cabinets, and even musical instruments, where practicable, are of the building itself, never fixtures upon it. No appliances or fixtures are to be admitted where circumstances permit the full development of the organic character of the building-scheme. Floor coverings are at least as much a part of the house as the plaster on the walls or the tiles on the roof.

Quoted in David A. Hanks. *The Decorative Designs of Frank Lloyd Wright.* New York: Dover, 1999, pp. 8–9.

The living room of the Wright-designed Hollyhock House. Wright believed that furnishings within a structure should be part of the architect's overall plan.

Wright incorporated most of these elements into the exterior of the Winslow House in River Forest, a village near Oak Park, in 1894. He was excited because the finished product was handsome and very livable. In addition, his unusual powers of perception regarding the state of architecture in America allowed him to catch glimpses of the profession's future. He correctly foresaw that the house's design and others similar to it would become models for millions of American homes in the coming century. "I will never forget the sensations [I had] when the Winslow House was built," he later remembered.

"All Oak Park and River Forest began prowling around the place," gawking at it for its novelty. "With that house, in the realm of [the family] residence modern architecture began to make its appearance in the United States." He added, "I remember the feeling aroused in me of wonder at the amazement and astonishment that house had created. It was the talk of the town."[25]

In 1895, the year following the construction of the Winslow House, Wright had eleven commissions for home designs, a large number for a single architect. The years that immediately followed witnessed the same high demand for his services. That popularity, coupled with his always hectic home life with the children, kept him constantly busy. Meanwhile Kitty, a bright, independent woman, was equally active, not only with child-rearing but also with arranging for the family's rich social life. As a result, the couple had little time to devote to their personal relationship and began to drift apart emotionally. This unfortunate trend would soon have serious consequences.

Open Floor Plans

Throughout these years Wright was constantly trying out new design ideas for the interiors of his houses. One that kept cropping up was a way to get away from the traditional tendency for floor plans to be cut up into a given number of separate rooms connected by one or more hallways. This approach has often been called, in a disparaging manner, "boxes within a box." He was already thinking about the concept of the then unheard-of open floor plan. Taken for granted today, it features some of the major rooms—typically the living room, dining room, and kitchen—flowing into one another with few or no separating walls.

A number of factors made this advance possible in the years when Wright was a young man. One of the most crucial was a new approach to heating homes. In the words of architectural historian Kathryn Smith, Wright realized that

> mechanized heating made it no longer necessary to close rooms off from each other to conserve heat. This

discovery led to the open plan in public spaces—for instance, where the living room opened to the dining room on a diagonal—while maintaining compartmentalized rooms for services. With the hearth no longer used as the major source of heat, Wright was free to liberate it from the wall and use it as a freestanding vertical plane in space. . . . By treating the fireplace as a solid screen that defined but did not enclose space, he created the free plan of modern architecture.[26]

Wright took a major step toward the open floor plan in his design for the Joseph J. Husser House, erected on the shore of Lake Michigan in Chicago in 1899. (Years later the city filled in the nearby stretch of lake to create more land for development, so the shoreline receded from the house by half a mile. Such "progress" eventually doomed the structure. In 1926 it was demolished to make way for an apartment building.) Wright used a cruciform layout, shaped like a cross, and allowed the rooms in two of the cross's four arms to flow into one another. The following year, his plan for the Susan Lawrence Dana House in Springfield, Illinois, also featured a cruciform. In this version, the open living area had a two-story ceiling, with a second-floor balcony overlooking the main space.

In 1901 Wright employed the cruciform concept still again, this time in his first major Prairie Home, the Ward W. Willits House in Highland Park (another Chicago suburb). About this visually striking structure art historian Trewin Copplestone writes,

This is a large house with servants' quarters, including a butler's pantry, on the ground floor, as well as an entry hall, living room, dining room, and kitchen. The upper floor includes three bedrooms, library, and nursery, and is roofed by a clear cruciform construction. . . . A calm and unified dignity emanates from the house, [which is] set on [a] concrete base that raises the living quarters above the spacious grounds. The structure is of

steel and wood, with plaster and exterior wood trim. . . .
The interior ground floor is a most effective expression
of Wright's desire to provide a continual spatial flow
and represents his personal response to the traditional
boxes within a box design.[27]

Wright's ultimate expression of the Prairie style in his initial period as an independent architect was the home he designed for bicycle manufacturer Frederick C. Robie in
Chicago in 1910. The exterior was composed of sandstone
slabs, wood, fired bricks, and glass. He left them all unpainted
and unadorned so that they blended organically with their
natural surroundings. As for the innovative interior, it was
built around a single axis, or central line to which the various

WALLS NO LONGER SOLID BARRIERS

One of the several major innovations that Wright's Prairie Houses introduced was the concept that a wall was no longer the solid bar-
rier it had traditionally been between the inside and outside of a house.
The Willets House was illustrative. In it, he subdivided the walls into a
group of design elements, among them flat planes, piers [upright sup-
ports], and furnishings around the windows. All of these were separated
or marked off by dark strips of wood placed in geometric patterns. "The
wall was now defined as an enclosure of space," architectural historian
Kathryn Smith points out. "Windows were no longer holes punched
through a mass, but a light screen filtering sunlight into the interior. The
movement outward toward the landscape was amplified by the addition
of porches, terraces, flower boxes, and planter urns."

Kathryn Smith. *Frank Lloyd Wright: American Master.* New York: Rizzoli, 2009, p. 39.

parts of the structure connected. Taking the open floor plan idea to its limits, the ground floor consisted of a living room separated from a dining room by a large central fireplace that people could walk around on both sides. Robin L. Sommer elaborates, saying that both ends of the central axis had

> projecting balconies and porches opening to the out-doors. There is no façade [front face, usual with the main entrance] on the street side, no visible entrance, and no ornamentation, as such. The single most arresting feature of the exterior is the cantilevered [projecting or overhanging] roof that extends 20 feet beyond its masonry [stone] supports. Inside, the large central living space . . . has no dividing walls or partitions—only a free flow of space richly embellished by burnished wood-work, patterned carpeting, art glass, French doors, and the broad recessed hearth. Bedrooms, kitchen, and servants' quarters are set to the rear of the house.[28]

The Larkin Building

In retrospect, Wright demonstrated his versatility as an architect, as well as his sheer energy, during this period of his career. While turning out one complex, brilliant house design after another, he also drew up the complicated plans for his first commercial structure. Darwin D. Martin, an executive at the Larkin Company, a successful mail order business in Buffalo, New York, had heard about Wright's modernistic homes. Martin hoped to persuade the controversial architect to design a large-scale administration building for the growing company. He explained to Wright that he and the owners of the business were progressives who strongly believed in creating humane, comfortable working conditions for their many employees. This compassionate attitude, rare among company owners at the time, intrigued Wright, and he agreed to take on the project.

Erected between 1903 and 1905, the Larkin Building was five stories tall and made of red brick. Its fortresslike exterior was highly geometrical with high rectangular towers topped by solid spheres. The entrance was flanked by fountains, while far above, the roof over the structure's central court was composed of glass. Carla Lind, former director of the Frank Lloyd Wright Building Conservancy (an organization that works to preserve existing structures he designed) describes the highly innovative interior:

> Magnesite, a durable poured concrete and wood product, was used to cover desktops, countertops, and floors. Sphere-within-a-square light fixtures, used individually and clustered, were mounted on walls and posts or suspended from the ceiling. Metal furniture was custom-designed for the record-keeping card system that Martin had devised. Many desks had swing-away chairs. Wooden and upholstered furniture was designed for the lounge, library, and dining areas. Windows were hermetically sealed and a clever cooling system kept the building comfortable. The acoustical [sound] plan was so successful that the central light court was amazingly quiet, despite the more than one thousand workers within the great space. The building included a rooftop terrace, conservatory, library, bakery, and restaurant.[29]

Oak Park's Unity Temple

While the Larkin headquarters was under construction, Wright accepted a commission for his first church. Ever since childhood, he had periodically attended the All Souls Unity Temple in Oak Park, a Unitarian church where his uncle Jenkin was the pastor. In June 1905 a fire destroyed the original structure, and the distraught congregation reached out to Wright.

To save his fellow parishioners money, he employed steel-reinforced concrete, then fairly inexpensive, in most of the exterior, giving it a slab-like, monolithic look. He also made the first story windowless to keep street noises from reaching the interior. This extremely unorthodox design for a church raised many eyebrows at first, as one scholar explains.

The Oak Park Unity Temple was Wright's first church design. The unorthodox monolithic exterior (top) drew criticism, but the church's interior (bottom) was praised.

The new building came as a considerable shock to the church authorities. It was like no other church that they had ever seen. Indeed, it is true to say that it was unlike any church that *anyone* had ever seen. It carried neither the familiar medieval or classical historicist elements and was, as Wright himself described it, "a concrete monolith."[30]

In contrast to the unexpected and unfamiliar exterior, the church's interior was warm and inviting. Copplestone writes,

> The quality of calm intimacy and a sense of spiritual peace is all-prevailing. It feels that it could not be other than it is—a place of worship. The effect of the roof lighting and the high side windows is restful and the soft colors and common identity of the whole decorative interior justifies the name Unity Temple.[31]

Wright himself elaborated on the lighting effects he had created for the structure's interior and their importance for making it seem so peaceful. "The interior space" is "enclosed by screen-features only," he jotted down on one of his drawings for the building.

> I flooded these side-alcoves with light from above to get a sense of a happy cloudless day into the room. And with this feeling for light, the center ceiling between the four great posts became skylight, daylight sifting through between the intersecting concrete beams, filtering through amber ceiling lights. Thus managed, the light would, rain or shine, have the warmth of sunlight.[32]

Uprooting Himself

Considering the excessive amounts of time Wright devoted to huge projects like the Unity Temple and Larkin Building, it is remarkable that he could squeeze out enough hours for a personal life. But somehow he did manage it. During the design and construction phases of these buildings, Wright was also

A CONTINUOUS OPENNESS

The inside of Wright's Robie House was seen as extremely innovative for its time, partly because of its design and also because Robie, a successful inventor, incorporated some of his own novel ideas. English art historian Trewin Copplestone provides this brief overview of the interior.

The low ground floor, visually minimized by the terrace walling of brick with a concrete top course emphasizing the horizontal, includes a children's playroom, billiard room, concealed entrance hall invisible from the street, boiler room, laundry, integral garages, and walled court[yard]. The living room, dining room, guest room, kitchen, and servants' quarters are on the first floor, with the master suite on the second partial story. The revolutionary element is that the ground- and first-floor main areas are unwalled so that a continuous flowing openness is only partially interrupted by the large chimney stack. Wright also designed all the fixtures and fittings, which . . . make the interior of exceptional interest. The house incorporates an additional number of inventive ideas contributed by Robie, such as an integrated industrial vacuum-cleaning system.

Trewin Copplestone. *Frank Lloyd Wright: A Retrospective View.* New York: Todtri, 2001, p. 40.

juggling his family duties to his wife and children and an extramarital affair with a woman named Mamah (MAY-muh) Cheney. He had met her in 1904 while designing a house in Oak Park for her and her husband, electrical engineer Edwin H. Cheney.

Like Kitty, Mamah was a smart, independent-minded woman. But she was neither more intelligent nor more attractive than Kitty. Exactly why Wright chose to jeopardize his marriage and personal reputation for a few stray hours with

Mamah remains unclear and has been the subject of much debate by biographers and historians over the years. Whatever the reasons were, in October 1909 she suddenly left her husband, and Wright asked Kitty for a divorce. Believing she could convince her husband to reconsider and save their marriage, Kitty said no. In response, he left home and took Mamah with him to Germany, where a publisher had asked him to compile a retrospective of his home designs. For the first time as an adult, Wright had uprooted himself, in the process reinventing his personal life. It would not be the last time he would do so.

From Taliesin to Tokyo: 1911–1923

Frank Lloyd Wright was often asked to define the art of architecture as he saw it, and he gave a number of answers over the years. One of them was: "Architecture is the triumph of human imagination over materials, methods, and men, to put man into possession of his own Earth. It is at least the geometric pattern of things, of life, of the human and social world. It is at best that magic framework of reality that we sometimes touch upon when we use the word order."[33] By this, he meant that architecture consists of putting natural materials in the proper physical order and in the process creating something worthwhile and lasting.

This definition could easily have been applied to any of the hundreds of structures Wright designed in his lifetime. But in particular, owing to his frequent use of the word *lasting*, it calls to mind an immense and unshakable building that sprang from his fertile imagination in the 1911–1923 phase of his career. This was the renowned Imperial Hotel in Tokyo, Japan. It was not only one of the largest structures he had ever designed, but also so well conceived and built that it proved capable of resisting the full brunt of nature's destructive fury.

That same period witnessed Wright's creation of another enormous building, this one in Chicago. No less enormous was

the breadth and pain of a sudden, terrible tragedy that turned his life upside down while that edifice was under construction. This personal calamity was so awful, in fact, that many ordinary people would never have recovered from it. But as one of the young architects that worked closely with him said, "Frank Lloyd Wright was no ordinary man."[34]

The Imperial Hotel in Tokyo, Japan, was designed by Wright to be virtually earthquake-proof.

A Nobleman's Villa

This simultaneously productive and heartbreaking period of Wright's life began on a bright note. Due to his separation from Kitty and ongoing relationship with Mamah, he moved out of the Oak Park house and needed a new place to live. For a long time he had been contemplating building a home on a plot of land his grandfather had settled in Spring Green many years before. Now he went about making it a reality, throwing his usual enormous energy into the project. As one of his modern biographers describes it,

> Wright began to build a princely compound on the shoulder of a hill in Spring Green. It was his fantastic version of an Italian nobleman's villa, designed expansively to embrace its own shops, studios, stables, homes, vineyards, lakes, pools and everything else that could make it self-sustainable. It was to be a fortress of beauty and sense against the gross world beyond the hills. Soaked in his own grandiose melodrama, he called it Taliesin. The name comes from a Welsh myth. A magical boy endured great suffering and grew into the poet-wizard Taliesin—in Welsh, "shining brow," for his broad, bright forehead.[35]

Wright's home, called Taliesin, sits on six hundred acres in Spring Green, Wisconsin, and ranks among the most innovative American architectural designs.

As Wright almost always did when approaching a new architectural design, he at first saw it in his mind's eye—both the exterior and interior—before ever approaching his drawing board. He later recalled,

> I saw the hill-crown [in the] back of the house as one mass of apple trees in bloom, [their] perfume drifting down the valley, later the boughs bending to the ground. . . . I saw plum trees, fragrant drifts of snow-white in the spring, loaded in August with blue and red and yellow plums. . . . I saw the vineyard on the south slope of the hill, opulent vines loaded with purple, green, and yellow grapes [and] bees humming all over [and] sheep grazing in the upland slopes. . . . Yes, [I saw that] Taliesin should be a garden and a farm behind a real workshop and good home. [It] was to be an abstract combination of stone and wood as they naturally met in the [nearby] hills. . . . Finished wood outside was the color of gray tree-trunks in violet light. Shingles of the roof surfaces were left to weather silver-gray like the tree branches spreading below them. Inside floors . . . were stone-paved or laid with wide, dark-streaked cypress boards. The plaster in the walls was mixed with raw sienna . . . drying out a tawny gold.[36]

The Colossal Midway Gardens

Wright, along with Mamah, moved into the spanking new Taliesin in December 1911. The press had recently had a field day with the scandal caused by their affair, which in that era was seen as more shameful than it would be today. As a result, some people who would normally have approached Wright to design for them opted to steer clear of him. Between 1912 and 1913 he received only six commissions, for him an unusually low number.

One of these projects, however, was of colossal size and scope, requiring him to hire a few young draftsmen to help draw up its complex plans. Called Midway Gardens, it was intended to be a combination of a beer garden and a modern entertainment center in the heart of Chicago. A beer garden, from the German *biergarten*, is traditionally an open area devoted to serving beer and local foods to large numbers of people. Edward C. Waller Jr., son of Wright's friend and former client Edward C. Waller, approached the architect, reminding him that beer gardens were then quite popular in Europe and North America. Waller envisioned merging the restaurants and eating areas with shops, arts galleries, a concert facility, a dance floor, and other popular attractions for public amusement.

Wright enthusiastically designed Midway Gardens in 1913, and its initial sections were erected the following year. Covering three acres, an entire city block, their overall look was reminiscent of Mayan or Aztec architecture, with solid stone masses rising in split-level horizontal layers. Unfortunately for all involved, however, the project was not successful. First,

This 1915 postcard view of Midway Gardens in the heart of Chicago shows the dance floor and hundreds of tables and chairs.

EXTRAORDINARY CREATIVE POWER

By the time Wright designed Taliesin in Wisconsin and Midway Gardens in Chicago, he had reached a much higher level of skill and ability than he had possessed as a young architect working for his mentor Louis Sullivan. Barry Byrne (1883–1967), a noted architect who as a young man assisted Wright from 1902 to 1908, eloquently explained this transformation.

The emergence of Wright as an architect in that period of his development when it was my good fortune to work under him also saw the recession [departure] of Wright as a draftsman. . . . He transformed himself from the more superficial precision of the draftsman type into a master architect whose occupation was no longer mere [technical drawing], but whose concern was that immeasurably greater thing, the large-scale manipulation of spaces and masses into a vital, intrinsic [native] architecture. . . . When I left the studio . . . Wright as a draftsman had almost ceased to exist and that more vital being, Wright as architect, was operating in full possession of his extraordinary creative power.

Quoted in Donald Hoffman. *Frank Lloyd Wright's Robie House: The Illustrated Story of an Architectural Masterpiece.* New York: Dover, 1984, p. 17.

Waller was plagued by personal financial problems and filed for bankruptcy only two years after the complex opened, forcing him to sell it to a brewery. (That company folded in 1928, and the following year the structures on the site were torn down. The large reinforced concrete buildings were so well conceived and built that two wrecking companies went out of business before a third managed to complete the demolition.)

Another reason that Wright was disappointed with Midway Gardens was that he encountered difficulties in bringing together all the artists and other specialized workers required to make the project a creative success. About this lack of overall integration of the various artistic elements, he later commented with considerable dismay, "I tried to complete the synthesis," or combination of the various design and decorative elements in a cohesive whole. "Planting [gardens], furnishings, music, painting, and sculpture [were] all to be one. But I found musicians, painters, and sculptors were unable to rise at that time to any such synthesis. Only in a grudging and dim way did most of them even understand [working so closely together] as an idea."[37]

A Madman's Nightmare

The thought of Midway Gardens triggered negative thoughts for Wright in his later years for another reason. In the summer of 1914, while overseeing some finishing touches on the project, he received the distressing news that Taliesin was on fire. Rushing to the scene, he found his worse fears confirmed. Much of the house had been destroyed by the blaze. But even worse, seven people had been killed, including Mamah, her two young children who had been visiting her, and four of Wright's draftsmen and friends.

Still more horrifying, the disaster had not been an accident. The house's butler, an apparently mentally unstable individual, had purposely set the fire. As the victims attempted to escape, he had cut them down with a small ax. In a final twist of fate, by sheer coincidence Edwin H. Cheney was on his way to pick up his children and arrived at the scene at the same time that Wright did. (The butler was found hiding in the house's boiler room the next day. He had tried to commit suicide by swallowing acid, which failed to kill him. Thereafter, he refused to eat and died several weeks later without explaining his motives for the awful deed.)

Not surprisingly, Wright was overwhelmed with shock and grief. He later recalled,

> Thirty-six hours earlier I had left Taliesin, leaving all
> [of its residents] living, friendly, and happy. Now the

blow had fallen like a lightning stroke. . . . In thirty minutes [most of] the house and all in it had burned to the stone work or to the ground. The living half of Taliesin was violently swept down and away in a madman's nightmare of flame and murder.[38]

For a short while, the devastated architect lived in a small rear portion of the house that had somehow escaped the flames. He tried to work on his designs but found it difficult because of the lingering horror of what had happened and his

The death toll from the Taliesin fire included Mamah Borthwick Cheney, pictured, her two children, and four of Wright's draftsmen and friends. Wright was devastated.

grief and pity for those who had lost their lives. He later recalled,

> The gaping black hole left by fire in the beautiful hill-
> side was empty, a charred and ugly scar upon my own
> life. . . . As I looked back at that time, I saw the black
> hole in the hillside, the black night over all. And I
> moved about in sinister shadows. Days strangely with-
> out light would follow the black nights.[39]

A Clever Strategy

Wright soon left the dismal ruins of his once happy home and
rented an apartment in Chicago while Taliesen was being re-
built. As the weeks rolled by, hundreds of notes and letters
flooded in, all expressing heartfelt sympathy for his tragedy.
One of them was from a sculptor named Maude Miriam Noel,
who preferred to be called Miriam. A skilled flatterer and social climber, she had set her sights on wooing Wright while he
was still shaken by his recent misfortune and emotionally vul-
nerable. Wright's biographer Jan Adkins says of her,

> It is difficult to write about Miriam Noel without mak-
> ing her sound like a cartoon. Her speech and writing
> were impossibly flowery, even by the standards of her
> day. . . . In her mid-forties, she was the widow of a de-
> partment-store businessman [and] accustomed to some
> wealth. . . . She had a Southern accent and a mysteri-
> ous, dramatic manner. Part of the mystery was certainly
> her enormous store of romantic illusions. She was a
> Christian Scientist, believed in ghosts and spirit medi-
> ums, attended séances, and was convinced that she
> could read others' thoughts and even the future. She
> was also convinced that her fate was to be part of a
> mythic love-bond with a famous artistic superman.
> Frank [Lloyd Wright] fit the fantasy.[40]

Wright viewed Miriam as moody and more than a little
odd. But for reasons only he knew, he found her hard to resist.

Within mere weeks of her initial letters to him, she had moved into the Chicago apartment with him. Later, in the summer of 1915, when the charred remains of the Spring Green house had been transformed into Taliesin II, she became his permanent house guest there, too.

She was with him later that year when he received word of a once-in-a-lifetime offer. The Japanese government had chosen him from among all the architects in the world to design its new

Imperial Hotel in Japan's capital city, Tokyo. The Japanese, whose culture harbored a deep reverence for the natural world, greatly respected his organic approach to architecture.

The massive project absorbed most of Wright's time and energies between 1915, when he began the design phase, and September 1923, when the hotel opened for business. No less crucial to him than the quality of the design was a concern for making the structure as resistant as possible to earthquakes. Japan is one of the most earthquake-prone countries in the world, and he felt it was imperative that the building be able to survive any quake, even a large one. This is why he spent

Shown here is the interior of the Tokyo Imperial Hotel lobby. Wright began planning the project in 1915, and the structure was completed in 1923.

countless hours pouring over the latest scientific research on seismology (the study of earthquakes) and examining hundreds of materials and techniques that might help to nullify the wave movements that travel through the ground during earthquakes. He later described some elements of the strategy he developed for the building, saying,

> Because of the wave movement, deep foundations, such as long piles, would oscillate and rock the structure. Therefore the foundation should be short or shallow. There was seventy feet of soft mud below the upper crust of eight feet of surface soil on the site of the Imperial Hotel. That mud seemed a good cushion to relieve the terrible shocks. Why not float the building upon it? A Battle-ship floats on salt water! And why not extreme lightness combined with . . . flexibility, instead of the great weight necessary to the greatest possible rigidity? Why not, then, a building made as the two hands thrust together, palms inward, fingers interlocking and yielding to movement, but resilient to return to its original position when distortion ceased? . . . Why fight the quake? Why not outwit it? That was how the building began to be planned.[41]

To make the building flexible and able to ride out a quake, Wright had workers drill holes in the ground all around at the building site. He filled the holes with concrete. Then, using heavy blocks of pig iron, he loaded down the pins, causing them to sink into the soil. Carefully measuring how far the pins sank, he calculated how much the heavy finished building would similarly settle and accordingly made the proper allowances in the plans. The result was a structure intended to float slightly within the soil when struck by subsurface earthquake waves.

What Wright Had Wrought

The effectiveness of Wright's design was proved with a vengeance. On September 1, 1923, the very day the building

ELIMINATING THE INSIGNIFICANT

While visiting Japan to oversee the planning stages of the Imperial Hotel, Wright studied a number of Japanese homes up close and was impressed by their simplicity and the attempt by their builders to make them architecturally organic. He later commented on it in his autobiography, saying in part:

I saw the native home in Japan as a supreme study in elimination of the insignificant. So the Japanese house naturally fascinated me and I would spend hours taking it all to pieces [in his head] and putting it together again. I saw nothing meaningless in the Japanese home and could find very little added in the way of ornament because all ornament, as we call it, they [acquire in] the way the necessary things are done or by bringing out and polishing the beauty of the simple materials they used in making the building. . . . Nothing is allowed to stand long as a fixture upon the sacred floors of any Japanese home. Everything the family uses is designed to be removed when not in use and be carefully put in its proper place . . . beautiful to use only when appropriate and use only at

the right moment. . . . At last I had found one country on Earth where simplicity, as natural, is supreme.

Frank Lloyd Wright. *Frank Lloyd Wright: An Autobiography.* Petaluma, CA: Pomegranate, 2005, p. 196.

Wright studied Japanese houses like this one and was impressed with their simplicity and with the elimination of insignificant details in their design.

opened, a monstrous quake—the biggest to hit Japan in modern history—struck Tokyo. More than 105,000 people died, and three-quarters of the city was flattened into mounds of rubble. Yet when the clouds of dust raised by the collapsing buildings cleared, the survivors saw that Wright's hotel was still standing—a heroic, magnificent sight rising above the ruins and a testament to the brilliance of its creator. In fact, the structure came through the tremors so well that the government used it to temporarily house some of the people who had lost their homes in the catastrophe.

Clearly, in both beauty and durability, Wright had wrought an architectural masterpiece. Soon after the disaster in Japan, his old mentor, Louis Sullivan, declared that the Imperial Hotel stood "unique as the high water mark thus far attained by any modern architect. Superbly beautiful; as it stands—a noble prophecy."[42]

4

Fallingwater Rising: 1924–1939

The decade and a half following the completion of the Imperial Hotel was, from a professional vantage, one of Frank Lloyd Wright's most productive and memorable periods. In it, he invented a completely new kind of home, the design of which became highly influential in America. He also created what came to be seen as the country's most famous house. The period was also quite turbulent for him from a personal standpoint.

The relatively short interval of 1923–1924, for example, proved to be one of the most eventful, unexpected, taxing, and distressing interludes of Wright's life. First, the quake had struck in Japan. Although the Imperial Hotel had survived, thereby eliciting raves about his skills from around the globe, the building's opening and intended use had to be delayed. Second, Wright's mother died in 1923, when he was fifty-six, causing him considerable sorrow. Next, his old mentor, Louis Sullivan, with whom he had reconciled in 1918, died early in 1924. Three weeks after Sullivan's passing, Miriam, whom Wright had wed late in 1922, suddenly left him for reasons that remain uncertain. She moved to Los Angeles, leaving him alone in Taliesin.

He did not remain alone for long, however. In November 1924 he attended a performance of Chicago's well-regarded ballet company and there met a beautiful woman. Aged twenty-six, three decades his junior, her name was Olga Iovanna Hinzenberg, but people always called her Olgivanna for short. She hailed from Montenegro in southeastern Europe and was divorced with one daughter, Svetlana. Once again, Wright quickly found himself smitten by strong romantic feelings, and in the spring of 1924 Olgivanna and her daughter moved into Taliesin with him.

After Miriam Noel left Wright in April 1924, he began seeing Olgivanna Hinzenberg, pictured with Iovanna, her child with Wright.

Taliesin III

As if this chain of important events had not been enough to disrupt Wright's life, soon after Olgivanna's appearance at Taliesin a second fire ravaged the house. This time it was caused by faulty telephone wires. Although a number of his antiques and architectural papers were lost in the blaze, Wright counted himself fortunate that no one had been killed or injured. He swiftly got to work designing and doing organizational work for Taliesin III.

This time around, Wright's reworking of Taliesin was partly inspired by suggestions made by the creative, strong-willed Olgivanna. Together, they envisioned the new Taliesin not simply as a comfortable residence resting amidst nature's beauty. They also wanted to create a gathering place and working environment for talented young architects who would learn from Wright while supplying him with the labor he required to manage the large compound's upkeep. Thus was born the Taliesin Fellowship. One of its number, John W. Geiger (1921–2011), remembered,

> [Wright] envisioned the Fellowship as a work force to accomplish his construction goals at Taliesin . . . and the establishment of an architectural office. . . . He had always had draftsmen working for him who were paid modest sums, if anything at all. The Fellowship apprentices needed to be conditioned to accept the realities of what it meant to be an apprentice to Frank Lloyd Wright. . . . The apprentices were neither students, nor employees, nor indentured servants, but apprentices, and reasonably intelligent individuals who knew, at least in general terms, what joining the Fellowship would require of them. This was no prison and the apprentice was free to leave at a time of his choosing. One friend left after the first weekend and another stayed a lifetime.[43]

The first recruits for the fellowship, which took time to organize properly, began arriving in October 1932. By that time,

In 2009 one of the young architects who became part of Wright's Taliesin Fellowship, John W. Geiger, looked back on that singular experience and evaluated its importance to him and the other apprentices, then and later in life.

For the apprentice it was an opportunity to participate in the creation of a world-class architecture and to observe a genius at work and play. It was a match made in heaven, or maybe hell, depending on your point of view. . . . There were no teachers at the Fellowship and no one was taught anything. If we learned anything at all, it was by the process of adsorption by being immersed in the Wright environment. . . . Whatever benefits were derived from being exposed to the "Wright" environment was up to the individual apprentice. What were the rewards? Primarily, at least superficially, it was architecture, architecture, and more architecture. . . . In the big picture, this probably worked more for the benefit of society than it did for Wright, the client, or the apprentices. As a part of the architectural environment were the two masterpieces of Taliesin and Taliesin West, and the reward of living in those environments on a daily basis. Was it worth it? Only the individual who participated can answer that question, but if you pose the question to those who participated, I think that you would find that the experience was, for the majority of the apprentices, the most important experience of their life.

John W. Geiger. "In the Cause of Architecture: Commentaries in Memoriam for Frank Lloyd Wright." http://jgonwright.com/ep01-fellow.html.

Wright had experienced several personal and professional milestones. Miriam, jealous of his happiness with Olgivanna, had tried to ruin his reputation, partly by suing them and also by stirring up scandals by leaking personal information about

The Willey House in Minneapolis, Minnesota, was the first of what Wright termed Usonian designs. They were smaller and more economical than typical Wright structures.

Wright to the press. These efforts largely failed. He and Olgivanna weathered the storm and married in August 1928. They had a daughter together, his seventh child, named Iovanna.

The Usonian Houses

Also by 1932 the country had slipped into a devastating financial slump known to history as the Great Depression. Following the collapse of the major stock markets in 1929, hundreds of banks had failed, millions of people had lost their jobs and/or life savings, and breadlines had become common in every American

city. In 1933 Democrat Franklin D. Roosevelt was sworn in as president (having been elected the preceding November). His administration emphasized that there was a serious need for affordable housing for millions of citizens who could not afford to buy or build even moderately expensive homes.

Wright responded to this appeal by coming up with new ideas in domestic architecture that could be implemented in low-cost ways. The first test for these ideas came in late 1933 and early 1934 with the Malcolm M. Willey House. A Minneapolis college professor, Willey approached Wright about designing a home for his family of modest means, and the architect, who saw it as an excellent opportunity to demonstrate his newest concepts, responded with enthusiasm.

The house became the earliest prototype for a new home design that Wright called Usonian, his acronym for "United States of America." A Usonian house was noticeably smaller than an average American home. It also saved on costs by ensuring that no interior space was wasted on nonpractical functions and that only low-cost, though still attractive, materials were used in construction. According to a noted expert on Wright and his buildings, the Usonian design

> recognized the changes taking place in American society and domestic life. . . . It was directed at an emerging lifestyle of a generation living a simpler, more mobile, and much less formal life. . . . The Usonian house was often L-shaped. It retained the traditional hearth and fireplace, but it dispensed with the formal dining room and the servants' wing. A dining area in the living room connected directly with the kitchen, where the two wings met. The bedroom wing, when set at an angle to the living quarters, framed an outdoor area serving both. A carport, which Wright also claimed to have invented, completed the Usonian design.[44]

The Willey House was experimental for Wright and as such utilized only some of his emerging Usonian-style concepts. The first home he designed that contained virtually all of these ideas was one he created in Madison, Wisconsin, in 1936 for

journalist Herbert Jacobs. The low-to-moderately priced home was composed mainly of brick, wood, and glass. Many elements were prefabricated, or prefab for short, meaning that they were pre-made and assembled at the work site. Its other main features included a single story; slab roof; board-and-batten walls; an uncomplicated planning grid; and a new kind of heating system in which electrical coils were embedded inside the concrete foundation.

Among the most important prefab elements that Wright used in his Usonian homes were so-called textile blocks, which he had developed several years before but had used only occasionally. (The first house that had employed them had been designed for California antique dealer Alice Millard in 1923.) The concrete blocks were fashioned in molds and bore decorative patterns that had been etched into the molds' surfaces. The idea was for a home owner to be able to install them him- or herself by

Millard House in Pasadena, California (opposite page and below), was the first design in which Wright utilized textile blocks. The blocks were fashioned in molds and bore decorative patterns on their surfaces.

placing them on a pre-marked grid on the flat poured concrete foundation. Held together with thin but strong steel rods, they could be stacked in any manner desired, allowing for considerable flexibility. Wright's goal, according to one authority,

> was to provide a custom-designed, fireproof dwelling filled with space and light. But to reduce the overall cost to the client, he introduced the machine-age concept of a standard unit and the radical notion of unskilled labor. His solution was a 16-inch-square concrete block with semi-circular grooves on four sides. To reduce the weight, the blocks were made concave, 3½ inches thick on their edges and 1½ inches in the middle. When placed end upon end and row over row, the grooves formed a cage of circular hollow channels, horizontally and vertically, throughout the wall. Slender steel rebar, measuring ¼ inch, was placed in these channels, which were filled with grout—resulting in a solid, monolithic wall. The essential grid of crisscrossed reinforced steel bars is what led to the title "textile block."[45]

An Environmental Embrace

In the same year that Wright designed the low-cost Jacobs House (1936), construction began on a much more lavish and expensive house he had conceived the year before for wealthy department store owner Edgar J. Kaufmann. The latter's son, Edgar J. Kaufmann Jr., had joined the Taliesin Fellowship in 1934 and soon afterward introduced Wright to his parents. Kaufmann Sr. told Wright that he and his wife were interested in building a weekend home on their large, wooded property in Mill Run, Pennsylvania. (Mill Run is the name of the local village. The house stands within the Bear Run nature preserve, which includes Bear Run stream.)

This house, known as Fallingwater, became not only Wright's most famous architectural work but also the most renowned and talked about house in the United States.

After seeing the setting, Wright decided he wanted to place the house directly over a breathtaking waterfall in a thick

Wright designed Fallingwater to sit over a waterfall and to blend with its environment. Many consider the house to be the ultimate expression of organic architecture.

stand of trees at one junction of the stream, then a revolutionary idea. He realized that this could make the structure his ultimate expression of organic architecture. That dream was fulfilled, as the house appears to grow directly out of its lush natural surroundings. Ada Louise Huxtable calls Fallingwater

> spectacularly and unconventionally beautiful. The familiar, much published view [seen in magazines and other media] shows a set of cascading horizontal concrete balconies dramatically suspended over a rushing waterfall, attached to the land by a vertical stone tower that contains an anchoring chimney and interior hearth. The house is so magically married to its site that it is thrilling to experience, and even to see. Wright's sense of the land is uncanny. He has locked building and setting together in a visual and environmental embrace. The effect is not of nature violated, but of nature completed—a dual enrichment.[46]

These words were echoed by the younger Kaufmann, who later said,

> To Wright, architecture was a great inclusive agency through which humankind adapted the environment to human needs and . . . attuned human life to its cosmos. Amid continual changes, architecture could keep human life more natural and nature more humane. This idea pervades Fallingwater in accord with the aims of both architect and client, and gives it not only basic meaning but also powerful subliminal [subconscious] appeal.[47]

A Momentous Decision

As the magnificent Fallingwater was rising in 1936, Wright was approaching seventy. As Jan Adkins says, he "seemed unstoppable, immortal, keeping up a furious jig of work, travel, writing, entertainments, and lectures. He tired out his apprentices and exhausted his clients."[48] Yet he had recently become aware that he was not in fact immortal. That winter he came down with a severe lung infection and as time went on he became

The "Background Music" at Fallingwater

Pulitzer prize–winner Ada Louise Huxtable, a leading American architectural critic, is one of the few people who can claim the distinction of having stayed overnight in Wright's most famous creation, Fallingwater. She later described the experience:

Most unforgettably, my husband and I were given the master bedroom directly over the falls, where light and sound rise from the water below. The house is on stepped levels, and the large downstairs living room has a surprisingly low ceiling, creating unexpected intimacy. Continuous casement windows lined with hand-woven fabrics and fur throws open to the views. A sheltering stone fireplace wall is flanked by a great anchoring boulder retained from the site. An open hatch in the polished stone floor leads down to the water beneath and a small natural pool. Here are Wright's eternal themes: fire, earth, and water, in perfect equilibrium. But what you are unprepared for is the sound. You hear water rushing softly, falling steadily, a kind of background music that stays with you as clearly as the image of the building. Designed and driven by its setting, Fallingwater fills the mind and the senses.

Ada Louise Huxtable. *On Architecture: Collected Reflections on a Century of Change.* New York: Walker, 2008, p. 205.

An interior view of Fallingwater. Both the interior and the exterior reflect Wright's harmonious themes of fire, earth, and water.

convinced that his health would be greatly improved by escaping the cold, damp Wisconsin winters and moving somewhere warm and dry.

The result was Wright's momentous decision to build a new home base in Arizona. He bought 800 acres (324ha) of land in the Sonoran Desert outside Scottsdale, and soon a caravan of cars and trucks—the fellowship on the move—made its way across the country. Thereafter, Wright, his family, and his apprentices most often spent their summers in the Spring Green Taliesin and their winters in the new Arizona house, which they dubbed Taliesin West. In Robin L. Sommer's words, the newest Taliesin was an organic masterpiece featuring

> massive base walls of desert masonry, surmounted by redwood frames and tent-like white canvas, like a sailing ship. The diffused light that came through the canvas softened the harsh glare of the sun and provided an ideal environment for both studio and living quarters. Strong diagonal slashes break the long straight axis of the complex,

In 1936 Wright moved to Scottsdale, Arizona, for his health. He built Taliesin West on eight hundred acres of land in the Sonoran Desert.

which is as one with the desert setting. Multicolored stone from the site was mixed with the concrete that forms its base walls and terraces. They contrast strikingly with the rich appointed interiors, with gold pile carpeting, woven textiles, hanging desert plants, native pottery—even a grand piano. Taliesin's living quarters are more like those of a legendary Arabian sheik than those of a rough-and-ready American frontier camp. . . . The tension inherent in Wright's lifelong quest for the ultimate synthesis [of a building and nature] was expressed at Taliesin West as almost nowhere else.[49]

Timeless Rather than Trendy

This same period witnessed Wright's creation of another large-scale commercial structure. This time he was approached by Herbert Johnson, president of the well-known Johnson's Wax Company, which made waxes, paints, and other products for maintaining buildings. It was one of the few American

AN UNEXPECTED WORK SPACE

Chicago-based architect and photographer Thomas A. Heinz, one of today's leading experts on Wright's buildings, provides this concise description of the unusual interior work space of the Johnson Wax Building, built between 1936 and 1939.

The interior of the main Administration building is unexpected. It is like looking through a small grove of concrete trees. The space is very large, but the columns create differing effects, at times making it appear larger and at others smaller—one of the dichotomies [divisions into two opposing parts] common to many Wright designs. The office furniture is innovative and certainly as modern as any of the time, yet it also has a timeless quality. The desks have three table levels, which could almost have been designed to accommodate today's computer keyboards and screens. Most of the chairs for those working on the main floor were three-legged, without wheel casters, and had pivoted backs. The colors of their original fabric covering included the familiar Cherokee red [one of Wright's favorite colors] of the floor and brick, along with a soft blue, green, and yellow ochre.

Thomas A. Heinz. *Frank Lloyd Wright: Field Guide.* Evanston, IL: Northwestern University Press, 2005, p. 198.

A work area in the Johnson Wax Building in Racine, Wisconsin, shows Wright's use of unique columns to create optical effects.

companies that had remained highly profitable throughout the Great Depression. Johnson wanted him to design a new administration building and research facility for the company in Racine, Wisconsin.

In his typical way, Wright approached the planning stage with the company workers' comfort in mind. As he had done in the Larkin Building many years before, he designed innovative furniture that, along with the project's exteriors, looked modern in a sort of timeless rather than trendy way. *Life*, then one of the country's best-selling magazines, commented, "Spectacular as the showiest Hollywood set, it represents simply the result of creative genius applied to the problem of designing the most efficient and comfortable, as well as beautiful, place in which Johnson Wax executives and clerks could do their work."[50]

Among the other innovative touches was the distinctive way that Wright planned for the windows and their transmission of light into the interior. What appear at a distance to be ordinary glass windows are something very different. Indeed, Thomas A. Heinz explains, the building

> has no plate glass windows, only [translucent] Pyrex glass tubes to admit light [only]. At night these become more pronounced, their luminosity making the roof appear to float above the red brick walls. The tubing not only serves to insulate the space, but also to prevent the workers from gazing out of the windows, daydreaming.[51]

The new Johnson Wax Building was completed in April 1939. At the age of seventy-two, when most architects were dead, retired, or far past their prime, Wright had once more triumphed. As one of his biographers quips, he had shaken "an astonishing and entirely new concept out of his sleeve" and created a "design for a new era in corporate architecture."[52] Surely, many people thought, he would make this remarkable feat his swan song and quit while he was ahead. After all, the conventional wisdom went, how many more brilliant architectural concepts could such an aged, increasingly frail person possibly produce? To the surprise of many, the answer turned out to be: quite a few.

5

A Temple of Spirit: 1940–1959

Professionally speaking, the final years of Wright's life were no less busy and productive than the earlier ones had been. In spite of his advancing age and increasing onset of health problems, he kept on going, taking on one project after another. Between 1940 and 1959, a whopping 234 homes and other buildings based on his designs were erected. In his seventies and eighties, he was outperforming nearly every other architect in the world, including those in the prime of their lives.

As for his personal life, it remained somewhat controversial but in a different way than in the past. Gone were the frequent stormy romances and related scandals. In their place came some unfortunate political fallout related to World War II, which began in Europe in 1939 and drew in the United States in 1941. Wright was a pacifist at heart. He detested the very idea of war and in a rather naïve, unsophisticated way assumed that there could never be any justification for nations to go to war with one another. He tended to stubbornly defend this attitude. As a result, at times he criticized the U.S. entry into the biggest conflict in human history. The vast majority of Americans, however, viewed their participation in the war as perfectly justified, since the Germans and Japanese were evidently seeking nothing less than world domination. So Wright's remarks were widely seen as unpatriotic, which hurt his public image.

With the end of the war in 1945, however, the country's mood changed dramatically, becoming optimistic, upbeat, and in general more forgiving of unpopular opinions. So many people were willing to give someone as brilliant and talented as Wright a second chance. As a result, the number of commissions he received each year, which had decreased during the war years, rebounded into a steady stream. "When the dark time was over," one of his biographers remarks, "Wright shone again."[53]

Units for the Masses

The leading edge of his popularity in the postwar years was in the low-cost housing market. There, his Usonian plan, along with designs by other architects based on it, accounted for a large proportion of the housing units for the masses erected during the huge home-building boom of the late 1940s. Many of the smaller houses in the boom were similar in size and layout to the one he had designed for Washington State newspaper reporter Loren Pope back in 1940.

Pope had been greatly inspired by reading the 1938 cover story about Wright in *Time* and longed to have a home designed by him. But because he was in the lower middle class,

In 1946 Wright designed the Usonian Pope-Leighey House in Falls Church, Virginia. It had a simple, open floor plan of less than twelve hundred square feet.

making only fifty dollars a week, he assumed that an architect of Wright's stature would never consider it. Still, Pope gave it a try. He gathered his courage and wrote to the architect, saying, "Dear Mr. Wright, there are certain things a man wants during life, and *of* life. Material things and things of the spirit. This writer has one fervent wish that includes both. It is a house created by you. Will you create a house for us? Will you?" Less than a month later, Pope was astonished when he received an answer from Wright, which said, "Dear Loren Pope: Of course I am ready to give you a house."[54]

The layout of the Pope House, built in Falls Church, Virginia, covered fewer than 1,200 square feet (111.5 sq m). Yet its simple, open floor plan imparted a feeling of much greater space. Adding to its comfort and charm was the amount of light let in through tall glass doors and windows and the Wright-designed furniture that was modular, meaning that it could be used in multiple ways. Pope was so happy with the house that he published an article praising both it and Wright in the August 1948 issue of *House Beautiful*. The article, titled "The Love Affair of a Man and His House," inspired large numbers of American couples to contact Wright in the 1940s and 1950s about having him design similar homes for them.

Among the few such queries that Wright had the time to answer and follow through on was one that led to the creation of the Isadore Zimmerman House in Manchester, New Hampshire. The Zimmermans wrote to him in 1949, and the Usonian house went up in 1952, with Wright's assistant, John W. Geiger, supervising the construction. Other inexpensive but distinctive and comfortable residences Wright designed in this period included the Louis B. Frederick House in Barrington Hills, Illinois, in 1954, and the Al Borah House in the same town, in 1957. The Al Borah House earned its share of notoriety for its extensive use of prefab materials. All were preselected, shipped on flatbed trucks, and assembled at the worksite. (Interestingly, Borah, the builder, never actually lived in the house. He used it as an exhibition home for the National Association of Home Builders, and the first actual resident, Frederick B. Post, bought it after the exhibition was over.)

Another of the Usonian houses built in the 1940s and 1950s was designed for Wright's youngest son, Robert Llewellyn Wright (1907–1985). Planned in 1953 and erected in 1957 in Bethesda, Maryland, it is unlike the average Usonian in that the outer walls follow curves and arcs called "hemicycles." These give it somewhat the shape of a football. Robert's brother, Lloyd (1890–1978), who was a successful landscape architect (and helped their father develop the textile block process), landscaped the house's grounds in 1960.

The Tree That Escaped

In the early 1950s, while he was busy turning out house designs, Wright was approached by Harold C. Price, the head of a successful Oklahoma oil pipeline and chemical company. Price said he was looking for an architect to design a new three-story headquarters building. The always persuasive Wright convinced him to expand the concept to nineteen stories, a much larger structure that would include shops and apartments as well as offices.

The Price Tower, as it came to be known, was completed in Bartlesville, Oklahoma, in 1956. Standing 221 feet (67m) tall, it is the only one of the several skyscrapers Wright designed that was actually built. The tremendous subsequent success of the building has been attributed to the fact that it strongly personifies or embodies Wright's lifelong belief that architecture should be organic. In advocating that human-made structures should be extensions of natural settings or objects, in this case he used as his model one of the most common and beautiful of all natural things—the tree. In fact, he nicknamed the Price Tower "the tree that escaped the crowded forest."[55] In the words of one expert observer,

> The Price Tower was conceived of as an enormous tree whose branches are broadly cantilevered floors emanating from a cross-shaped supporting spine. Beginning with a rotated square divided into four quadrants, Wright developed the pinwheel geometry of the Price

Tower, which generated everything from the building's floor plans and construction details to its elevations and ornament. This geometry was the first of its type to be used, replacing the designs of a conventional steel frame. This hollow concrete spine contains all the building's plumbing, elevators, and air-conditioning systems and breaks the structure into four quadrants. Three of the quadrants were designed to be used as office spaces, and the remaining quadrant for duplex apartments. The vertical central core absorbs the weight of each successive floor, similar to how a trunk supports the branches of a tree.[56]

Wright's Price Tower in Oklahoma was the only skyscraper he designed that was actually built. Completed in 1956, with a design inspired by tall trees, it stands 221 feet high.

The Guggenheim Museum

Wright designed another important large-scale structure in his final years—the Guggenheim Museum in New York City. It was first conceived in the 1940s when millionaire art lover Solomon R. Guggenheim commissioned him to create a building to house his enormous collection of modern art. The project encountered several delays over the years. These included the scarcity of resources during World War II and the difficulty of finding a suitable site in the years following the conflict. Ground was finally broken in August 1956, and the building opened in October 1959, a few months after Wright's death.

In the same way that the Price Tower imitated a tree, the Guggenheim mimicked another natural form—the spiral, or helix, which is seen, for example, in the shells of nautiluses and snails. At one point Wright joked, "I have found it hard to look a snail in the face since I stole the idea of his house—from his back. The spiral is so natural and organic a form for whatever would ascend that I did not see why it should not be played upon and made equally available for descent at one and the same time."[57]

This use of the word *descent* was a reference to the manner in which the building's spiral is employed. Its concept of a rotunda, or circular ground plan, was, as in Wright's other buildings, designed to make form follow function. In this case, he felt that a circular form would fit the needs of the museum's visitors by providing them with a highly educational experience. Kathryn Smith explains his reasoning, saying,

> The main rotunda was conceived as a huge upended vessel with a ramp spiraling down from a centrally placed translucent glass dome. The museum visitor was instructed to take the elevator to the top, and then to proceed to view the art collection in a downward circular motion, pausing at each level to gain insight and cosmic awareness, thereby arriving back on the ground a more enlightened individual than before.[58]

For his design of the Guggenheim Museum in New York City, Wright drew inspiration from the shells of nautiluses and snails. The renowned museum opened in 1959, a few months after Wright's death.

This basic concept for the central core of the museum worried a number of artists and art critics before the Guggenheim opened. They questioned the practicality of visitors standing on a downward-slanting surface while trying to study an artwork. They also criticized the notion of hanging flat paintings on a curved wall. These concerns later proved trivial, however. Although a few people still have such misgivings, the overwhelming judgment of the art world and public alike has been that Wright's design is both fascinating and appropriate. When she had first met with Wright in 1943, the museum's curator, Hilla Rebay, had told him she wanted him to create "a temple of spirit."[59] Many people feel he achieved that goal in admirable fashion.

A Design of Beauty and Reverence

Wright created a temple of a different sort that was also completed in 1959. In 1953 Mortimer Cohen, rabbi of the Beth Sholom Synagogue in Elkins Park, Pennsylvania, wrote to him. The congregation wanted to erect a new synagogue to replace the one built in 1922, Cohen said, and desired to know whether Wright would design it.

After the architect agreed, the rabbi told him what he had in mind for the exterior of the edifice. He hoped it would capture the spirit of the summit of Mt. Sinai, the sacred mountain on which, according to the Bible, God delivered the Ten Commandments to Moses. Working with this concept, Wright conjured up a revolutionary upward-sloping triangular roof studded with large panes of translucent glass. These panes were intended to flood the structure's interior with filtered sunlight, creating the feeling of a heavenly glow. Delighted beyond measure, after receiving the initial designs Cohen telegraphed Wright. "Sketches arrived safely," he said. "All [of us are] deeply inspired by their beauty and majesty. You have taken the supreme moment in Jewish history and experience—the revelation of God to Israel through Moses at Mt. Sinai—and you have translated that moment with all it signifies into a design of beauty and reverence."[60]

BUILDING IN THE IMAGINATION

When Wright was alive, people often asked him about his working methods and where he derived his ideas. His stock answer was that he first envisioned his designs in his mind, as he explained in an interview:

[I] conceive the buildings in imagination, not first on paper, but in the mind. . . . [I] let the building . . . develop gradually, taking more and more definite form before committing it to the drafting board. When the thing sufficiently lives for you, then start to plan it with instruments, not before. . . . Construct and complete the building so far as you can before going to work on it with the T square and triangle. . . . If [the] original concept is lost as the drawing proceeds, throw away all and begin afresh.

Quoted in Ben Raeburn and Edgar Kaufmann, eds. *Frank Lloyd Wright: Writings and Buildings.* East Rutherford, NJ: New American Library, 1987, p. 221.

Although by this time he had become frail and walked with the assistance of a cane, Wright managed to visit the synagogue's construction site in January 1959. He was pleased to see that most of the roof and glass panels had been installed. This unfailing dedication to work and duty, no matter the personal discomforts, remained one of his hallmarks. Indeed, regardless of his advanced years he never retired, nor did he reduce his workload significantly. This was in spite of the fact that he began to suffer from Ménière's disease when he was about ninety. An inner-ear disturbance, it causes periods of dizziness, headaches, nausea, and vomiting.

When these symptoms were not present, however, he claimed to feel perfectly fine and seemed able to enjoy the pleasant atmosphere maintained for him at his Taliesin compounds by Olgivanna and his apprentices. According to a *New York Times* article written in that period,

> He continued to live his later years, much as the earlier ones, hard at work [and] teaching at Taliesin with sixty-five architectural students. Working a full day, he emerged [in the evening] often to make a public appearance in flowing tie, white hair under a porkpie hat, and to make a characteristic utterance [brief statement].[61]

His Inner Light

What appeared to be a minor health issue occurred in the spring of 1959. Suffering from an intestinal obstruction, Wright agreed to go to a hospital in Phoenix, where a surgeon removed the blockage. However, by this time his constitution had apparently become so weak that the recovery was simply too much for him. Death claimed Frank Lloyd Wright on April 9, 1959, when he was just two months shy of his ninety-second birthday.

Longtime friend Wes Peters drives a farm wagon containing Wright's coffin to a family cemetery not far from the architect's Taliesin home in Wisconsin.

WRIGHT'S AVERSION TO BASEMENTS

Wright's Usonian homes, like his Prairie Houses, had no basements. He presented his argument against basements in a 1954 essay titled "The Natural House."

A house should—ordinarily—not have a basement. In spite of everything you may do, the basement is a noisome, gaseous, damp, place. From it come damp atmospheres and unhealthful conditions. Because people rarely go there—and certainly not to live there—it is almost always sure to be an ugly place. The family tendency is to throw things into it, leave them there, and forget them. . . . Another objection to the basement is that it is relatively expensive. It has to be some six to eight feet below grade and so you have to get big digging going. It is a great inhibition in any building because you must construct a floor over it and the space it provides you with is, as I have said, usually disreputably occupied.

Quoted in Bruce B. Pfeiffer, ed. *The Essential Frank Lloyd Wright: Critical Writings on Architecture.* Princeton, NJ: Princeton University Press, 2008, p. 353.

Wes Peters, a former apprentice who had become an architect and close friend, immediately drove the coffin bearing the body of his mentor across the country to Taliesin III in Spring Green. There, he and some other friends loaded the casket onto a farm wagon. The next day around forty family members and friends walked solemnly behind the wagon as it was driven to the small family cemetery lying a few hundred yards from the house. Then they buried Wright beside his mother and Mamah Cheney.

The physical version of Frank Lloyd Wright had departed. But his spirit remained in the living beauty of the buildings he had designed and the influence of his ideas on future architects. He foresaw that this spiritual version of himself would survive his passing and alluded to it in one of his last writings, "A Testament," in 1957. He said in essence that an artist's humanity shines through in the beauty of his creations, which often outlive him. He defined that humanity as an inner light. "Sunlight is to nature as this interior light is to man's spirit," he wrote, adding, "There is nothing higher in human consciousness than beams of this interior light. We call them beauty."[62]

The Light That Never Fails

A s one of the most influential architects of all time, Frank Lloyd Wright left behind a cultural legacy of enormous proportions. Historian William Cronon remarks, "I don't think it's unfair to say that there is no American architect who has ever lived who has done as much to touch the world, who has done as much to realize his vision of what a perfect architecture might be than Frank Lloyd Wright."[63]

The chief modern proponent of organic architecture, Wright inspired thousands of other architects and builders across the world. To one degree or another, they employed his principles that make a building as much as possible an outgrowth of nature rather than something artificial that is simply placed there. He also introduced or popularized many architectural design concepts, of which a number are still in wide use. One of these contributions, a researcher points out,

> was the idea of using unfinished materials. Wright would construct walls of boulders or rocks from around the building sites without ruining the natural beauty of the rock. He also popularized the use of concrete as a building material. He used windows to decorate and accentuate the outdoors and to assist in heating, supporting his

WRIGHT: THE GREAT MOUNTAIN

Architectural observer and critic Paul Goldberger said this about Wright's importance to the field of architecture:

If you're a composer, I presume you don't want to sit down and write a symphony that sounds like Beethoven's. But how can Beethoven not be an immense part of the legacy of the art that you devote your life to? And so it is in architecture with Frank Lloyd Wright. There is this immense presence [of his], this great mountain and even if you want to make your own world on the other side of it, you have to climb it and understand it. . . . Frank Lloyd Wright is the great mountain of late 19th and early 20th century architecture. And you have to climb it if you want to go anywhere else. . . . Wright was a vast figure. He was enormous. [He] bridged time, space, styles, he transformed himself constantly throughout this long career which went through phase after phase and type after type. He seemed to do absolutely everything. . . . He was large, he was many-sided, he was many different things at many different times. The only real figure in the world of the arts that equaled him in the twentieth century, I think, was [the great painter] Picasso, [who was] another figure with . . . its legs planted in the nineteenth century but the body did this great jump into the twentieth century.

Quoted in PBS. "Frank Lloyd Wright: Legacy." http://www.pbs.org/flw/legacy/index.html.

A 1942 photo shows Frank Lloyd Wright at work in his office. A giant in American architecture, Wright was tireless in his quest to develop innovative designs.

goal of form fits function. He was also the first to use roof overhangs to help with heating and cooling. The overhangs would block the sun in the summer, while letting it in during the winter when the sun is lower in the sky. With his Prairie Style, he introduced asymmetrical floor plans like the open floor plan.[64]

In addition to inspiring large numbers of architects he had never met, Wright also directly trained or employed dozens of them. Some worked as his assistants in Oak Park and/or the Spring Green Taliesin compound, while others were part of the apprentice program he ran at Taliesin West. Among those who later achieved notoriety and success were Antonin Raymond, Barry Byrne, William E. Drummond, Marion M. Griffin, Aaron Green, Richard Neutra, John Lautner, and Henry Klumb.

Maintaining Wright's Houses

Certainly no small part of Wright's legacy was his astoundingly large output of houses, businesses, office buildings, and other structures that are still standing today. Some, like the Guggenheim Museum and Price Tower, remain in use, while many others have become national historic landmarks. The latter are maintained by public or private organizations and open to visitors who come from far and wide to experience them in person. Fallingwater, for example, originally built for Edgar J. Kaufmann, is overseen by the Western Pennsylvania Conservancy. "The impression one gets when touring the building," Thomas A. Heinz writes, "is that the Kaufmanns have left for the day, allowing others to enjoy their house, including the display of fresh flowers, fruit, and current magazines on the tables. Much of the furnishings are original, as is the art."[65] Meanwhile, Wright's original home and studio in Oak Park are owned by the National Park Service and managed by the Frank Lloyd Wright Preservation Trust.

In contrast, some of Wright's other structures, most of them family residences, were not well maintained after his death and subsequently fell into varying states of disrepair. In the cases of an undetermined number, fortunately, younger architects and

nonarchitects alike bought and restored them. In the process, they created new expressions of Wright's original architectural visions that have become models of well-ordered home design for new generations of Americans.

In 1975, for example, Philadelphia architect Albert H. Clark and his wife, Georgianna, bought the Sweeten House in Cherry Hill, Pennsylvania, a Usonian home designed by Wright in 1950. Impressed by his initial inspection of the structure, Clark remarked, "This house is more contemporary than most architects build today!"[66] After refurbishing the house, the Clarks have found it to be most efficient as well as comfortable. Their single complaint is that the fireplace smoked a bit too much, compelling them to seal it off. Robin L. Sommer points out that "the heirs to Wright's legacy consider these minor inconveniences as nothing compared to the pleasures of living in a work of art."[67]

Fallingwater is overseen today by the Western Pennsylvania Conservancy. Thousands of visitors tour the house annually.

Rolling with the Punches

Wright's importance as a creative artist and thinker also rested upon his refusal to allow advancing technology to dictate how he should think, work, and act. He looked around and saw

HOUSES NOT SO LIVABLE?

A few modern observers of Wright's works and legacy have been less kind than the majority. Although they do not deny that Wright's ideas were revolutionary, brilliant, and important, they feel that many of his houses turned out to be less practical than the architect's clients, and Wright himself, had hoped they would be. One such critic asserts:

[W]right's] modernistic houses didn't work very well. Inevitably, flat roofs leaked (Wright once said that if the roof doesn't leak, the architect hasn't been creative enough). Built-in furniture limited the uses to which rooms could be put, and a total design that included movable furniture militated against bringing your own furniture inside. (When visiting the homes of his clients, Wright was known to move "his" furniture back where it belonged.) Angles that were anything but ninety degrees made it difficult to add or expand rooms as desired in order to meet new needs. (Several of Wright's clients simply ordered a new house when they outgrew the old one.) The use of new, untried materials complicated maintenance and improvement. As a result, many houses by Frank Lloyd Wright are no longer family homes but museums lovingly (and expensively) cared for by non-profit trusts and foundations. In short, these machines for living often turned out to be not so livable.

Peter Saint-Andre. "The House that Rand Built." http://books.stpeter.im/rand/house.html.

what he believed were both artists and ordinary people losing touch with nature and its simplicity and beauty because of increased reliance on machines and other forms of technology. It was better for humans to use technology wisely and control it, rather than be controlled by it, he said. That philosophy, which stood out as fresh and bold in the growing machine age, inspired thousands of people, especially architects and other artists, to keep in touch with nature and the simpler aspects of life in both their work and leisure time. As always, this philosophy of life rested firmly on the foundation of his interpretation of organic architecture. "Man takes a positive hand in creation whenever he puts a building upon the Earth beneath the sun," he wrote.

> If he has a birthright at all, it must consist in this—that he, too, is no less a feature of the landscape than the rocks, trees, bears, or bees of that nature to which he owes his being. . . . The sum of man's creative impulses, we find, took substance in architecture as his creative passion rose and fell within it. . . . Of what use to us are miraculous tools until we have mastered the humane, cultural use of them? We do not want to live in a world where the machine has mastered the man; we want to live in a world where man has mastered the machine![68]

Though most people would agree with this and Wright's other insights about the evolution of modern technology and art, a few disagree with his basic approach to architecture. Over the years critics have called attention to the fact that his frequently flat roofs had a tendency to leak. Also, the Clarks were not the only residents of Wright-designed homes to complain about smoking fireplaces. Another objection has been that his custom-designed furnishings sometimes made it difficult for owners to rearrange furniture and other items.

Most modern historians, along with art critics and lovers, brush such negative evaluations aside, however. They argue that even if Wright's houses do not or cannot please everyone, large numbers of people would benefit from and enjoy living in a Wright-designed home. As Ada Louis Huxtable puts it,

> Not everyone loved [his houses] or were converted to [his] ideas about living. Over the years, there have been owners who have felt imprisoned by their [Wright-designed] houses, acting as Wright's reluctant caretakers. . . . But Wright's houses never insisted that their occupants reshape

themselves to conform to an abstract architectural ideal. . . . Usonian houses were, and are, inviting and livable. Those who commissioned them knew what they were getting, and, even when they received the unexpected . . . they rolled with the punches.[69]

Carla Lind agrees. "Wright's buildings have proven their relevance," she says. "Informal, environmentally sensitive, and based on a close relationship with the earth, these masterworks demand our respect along with our care."[70]

Cities of the Future

However long Wright's existing buildings may last, they were not the only ones he designed. At least half of his architectural conceptions were never actually built for one reason or another, and some of those that have survived remain inspiring visions for humanity's future. Indeed, among the many creative roles Wright played was that of visionary. Many of his ideas were not only state-of-the-art but often far ahead of their time. When not working on paid commissions, he spent considerable time describing, sketching, and in some cases actually designing buildings and entire cities that he hoped would be constructed in the future.

Regarding those future cities, he insisted that they should not be the chaotic, dirty, frequently dehumanizing places that many American urban areas had become. Instead, he stressed, they should be simpler, more sleek and elegant, and cleaner. In one of his more eloquent descriptions of a future city, he said,

> Imagine a city iridescent [gleaming] by day, luminous by night, imperishable! Buildings, shimmering fabrics, woven of rich glass; glass all clear or part opaque and part clear, patterned in color or stamped to harmonize with the metal tracery that is to hold all together, the metal tracery to be, in itself, a thing of delicate beauty consistent with slender steel construction, expressing the nature of that construction in the mathematics of structure, which are the mathematics of music as well.

Such a city would clean itself in the rain, [and] would know no fire alarms. . . . To any extent the light could be reduced within the rooms by screens, blinds, of insertion of translucent or opaque glass. The heating problem would be no greater than [it is in current structures] because the fabric [of the buildings] would be mechanically perfect, the product of the [state-of-the-art] machine shop. . . . I dream of such a city. I have worked enough on such [buildings] to see definitely [their] desirability and practicability.[71]

Wright's work on futuristic cities began in 1932 with his publication of *The Disappearing City*. The book advocated the

Wright reviews the model of his remarkable Broadacre City design for suburban development. Wright's concept was to relocate city inhabitants to smaller, cleaner communities in the countryside.

daring idea of breaking up some of the existing crowded cities and relocating their inhabitants in smaller, cleaner communities in the countryside. Two years later he introduced a 12-foot-square scale model (3.7m square) of one of these rural communities, called Broadacre City. The model toured the country in 1945. Wright released an updated version of the 1932 book in 1958, the year before his death, renaming it *The Living City*. For this version, he and his apprentices created numerous sketches showing futuristic minicities in rural settings.

The boldest of all the futuristic concepts Wright produced was his now renowned mile-high (1.6 km-high) skyscraper. In the 1950s someone approached him about designing a mile-high TV tower and he felt that it would be a waste to have such a tower without a building holding it up. So in August 1956 he created a rendering of a superb, sleek skyscraper, dubbed the "Illinois." As depicted in his sketches, its 528 stainless steel stories rise more than 5,000 feet (1,524m) into the sky, gradually tapering to a needlelike pinnacle. For structural integrity, he proposed layers of cantilevered stories connected to a vertical central core, as in his Price Tower. For extra strength, he added powerful cables like those in suspension bridges. Each connects the outer edge of a story to the one above it. The proposed building has some 18 million square feet (1.67 million sq. m) of floor space and enough volume and interior facilities to accommodate one hundred thousand people, fifteen thousand cars, and one hundred helicopters. In another far-thinking gesture, the elevators glide upward under atomic power.

Masters of Their Environment

Wright's magnificent Illinois was never built, of course. But it *could* become a reality if a person or organization would invest the necessary funds. The proof can be seen in Dubai, a sprawling city in the small Middle Eastern nation of the United Arab Emirates. In 2010 a 0.5-mile-high skyscraper (0.8km), the Burj Khalifa, designed by the Chicago firm of Skidmore, Owings, and Merrill, opened in Dubai. Closely resembling the Illinois, it cost an estimated $1.5 billion. It demonstrates clearly that

Wright's bold concept of a mile-high skyscraper was never built, but—at about half a mile high—the Burj Khalifa skyscraper in Dubai, United Arab Emirates (pictured), demonstrates that today's engineers have developed the technology to build such towering structures.

engineers and builders have attained the technology required to raise such towering structures, just as Wright insisted they would more than half a century ago. So perhaps his mile-high masterpiece will someday become a reality.

For the present, what is certain is that Wright's legacy to architecture, the building industry, and residential living is firmly implanted in the fabric of modern society and life. Virtually every town in the United States contains at least some homes or commercial structures employing concepts he introduced. As one expert phrases it, "There was never an architect who did as much for as long, or one who affected more people."[72]

As a result, Wright achieved his most cherished goal. More than anything else, he wanted to use architectural ideas to change the way people lived, in the process improving humanity's overall condition. In fact, he believed that one of his main duties as an artist—more specifically an architect—was to help his fellow humans to reach their highest potential while becoming masters of their environment. He called architecture, art, and religion "the inspired work of mankind." Thanks to them, he held, humans radiate a symbolic light, one that cannot be seen by the eye, but which is reflected in the beauty of their finest creations. If people continue to have great buildings, great art, and deep faith, he seemed to say, "we may call humanity itself the light that never fails."[73]

Notes

Introduction: The Arrogance of the Brilliant

1. Quoted in KCC Big Country. "Frank Lloyd Wright: A Man Far Ahead of His Time." HubPages. http://kccbigcountry.hubpages.com/hub/Frank-Lloyd-Wright-A-Man-Far-Ahead-of-His-Time.

2. Franklin Toker. *Fallingwater Rising: Frank Lloyd Wright, E.J. Kaufmann, and America's Most Extraordinary House.* New York: Knopf, 2004, pp. 30–31.

3. Quoted in Unity Temple Restoration Foundation. "Philosophy." www.utrf.org/philosophy.html.

4. Quoted in Herb Sosa. "Rediscovering an American Treasure in Pasadena: Frank Lloyd Wright's Millard House." www.ambiente.us/05010FLW.html.

5. Frank Lloyd Wright. Interview by Mike Wallace. "The Mike Wallace Interview," September 1, 1957, and September 28, 1957. Video. Harry Ransom Center, University of Texas at Austin. www.hrc.utexas.edu/multimedia/video/2008/wallace/wright_frank_lloyd_t.html.

6. Quoted in Architectural World. "Architectural Presentation: Frank Lloyd Wright," April 2008. http://architectural-world.blogspot.com/2008/04/architectural-presentation-frank-lloyd.html.

7. Wright. "The Mike Wallace Interview."

8. Quoted in Bruce B. Pfeiffer, ed. *The Essential Frank Lloyd Wright: Critical Writings on Architecture.* Princeton, NJ: Princeton University Press, 2008, p. 319.

9. Ken Burns. "The Master Builder." *Vanity Fair,* November 1998, p. 303.

10. Quoted in Burns. "The Master Builder," p. 318.

Chapter 1: Journey to Oak Park: 1867–1893

11. Frank Lloyd Wright. *Frank Lloyd Wright: An Autobiography.* Petaluma, CA: Pomegranate, 2005, p. 11.

12. Robin L. Sommer. *Frank Lloyd Wright: American Architect for the Twentieth Century.* Greenwich, CT: Brompton, 1993, p. 10.

13. Wright. *Frank Lloyd Wright: An Autobiography*, p. 105.

14. Chicago History Museum. "Louis Sullivan at 150: Invitation." www .sullivan150.org/about/invitation.php.

15. Quoted in Edgar Kaufmann, ed. *Frank Lloyd Wright: An American Architecture*. San Francisco: Pomegranate, 2006, p. 260.

16. Quoted in Randolf C. Henning. *Frank Lloyd Wright's Taliesin*. Madison: University of Wisconsin Press, 2011, p. 5.

17. Thomas A. Heinz. *Frank Lloyd Wright: Field Guide*. Evanston, IL: Northwestern University Press, 2005, p. 292.

18. Quoted in Ada Louis Huxtable. *Frank Lloyd Wright*. New York: Viking, 2004, pp. 67–68.

Chapter 2: Homes in the Prairie: 1894–1910

19. Quoted in Unity Temple Restoration Foundation. "Philosophy."

20. Toker. *Fallingwater Rising*, p. 18.

21. Quoted in Pfeiffer. *The Essential Frank Lloyd Wright*, p. 416.

22. Toker. *Fallingwater Rising*, p. 20.

23. Frank Lloyd Wright. "Organic Architecture." *Architects' Journal*, August 1936, p. 182.

24. Quoted in Pfeiffer. *The Essential Frank Lloyd Wright*, pp. 35–36.

25. Quoted in Kaufmann. *Frank Lloyd Wright: An American Architecture*, pp. 66–67.

26. Kathryn Smith. *Frank Lloyd Wright: American Master*. New York: Rizzoli, 2009, pp. 38–39.

27. Trewin Copplestone. *Frank Lloyd Wright: A Retrospective View*. New York: Todtri, 2001, p. 31.

28. Sommer. *Frank Lloyd Wright: American Architect for the Twentieth Century*, p. 18.

29. Carla Lind. *Lost Wright: Frank Lloyd Wright's Vanished Masterpieces*. New York: Simon and Schuster, 1996, p. 35.

30. Copplestone. *Frank Lloyd Wright: A Retrospective View*, pp. 38–39.

31. Copplestone. *Frank Lloyd Wright: A Retrospective View*, p. 39.

32. Quoted in Bruce B. Pfeiffer. *Frank Lloyd Wright, 1867–1959: Building for Democracy*. Los Angeles: Taschen, 2006, p. 27.

Chapter 3: From Taliesin to Tokyo: 1911–1923

33. Quoted in Unity Temple Restoration Foundation, "Philosophy."

34. John W. Geiger. "In the Cause of Architecture: Commentaries in Memoriam for Frank Lloyd Wright." http://jgonwright.com/ep01-fellow .html.

35. Jan Adkins. *Up Close: Frank Lloyd Wright*. New York: Viking, 2007, p. 117.

36. Quoted in Huxtable. *Frank Lloyd Wright*, pp. 129–132.

37. Quoted in Kaufmann. *Frank Lloyd Wright: An American Architecture*, p. 60.

38. Quoted in Henning. *Frank Lloyd Wright's Taliesin*, p. 50.

39. Quoted in Henning. *Frank Lloyd Wright's Taliesin*, p. 54.
40. Adkins. *Up Close*, pp. 133–134.
41. Wright. *Frank Lloyd Wright: An Autobiography*, pp. 214–215.
42. Louis Sullivan. "Reflections on the Tokyo Disaster." *Architectural Record*, February 1924, p. 119.

Chapter 4: Fallingwater Rising: 1924–1939

43. Geiger. "In the Cause of Architecture."
44. Huxtable. *Frank Lloyd Wright*, pp. 202–203.
45. Smith. *Frank Lloyd Wright: American Master*, pp. 142–143.
46. Huxtable. *Frank Lloyd Wright*, p. 203.
47. Edgar Kaufmann Jr. *Fallingwater: A Frank Lloyd Wright Country House.* New York: Abbeville, 2001, p. 31.
48. Adkins. *Up Close*, p. 208.
49. Sommer. *Frank Lloyd Wright: American Architect for the Twentieth Century*, p. 122.
50. Quoted in Pfeiffer. *Frank Lloyd Wright, 1867–1959*, p. 57.
51. Heinz. *Frank Lloyd Wright: Field Guide*, pp. 197–198.
52. Adkins. *Up Close*, pp. 238–239.

Chapter 5: A Temple of Spirit: 1940–1959

53. Adkins. *Up Close*, p. 262.
54. Quoted in Carol Hutchinson. "College Consultant Loren Pope; Commissioned Wright House." *Washington Post*, September 27, 2008. www.washingtonpost.com/wp-dyn/content/article/2008/09/26/AR2008092603547.html.
55. Quoted in Price Tower Arts Center. "From Design to Construction." http://pricetower.org/about-ptac/prairie-skyscraper/design-to-construction.
56. Quoted in Urbane Chaos. "Frank Lloyd Wright in Oklahoma: The Price Tower." http://urbane-chaos.hubpages.com/hub/FrankLloydWrightPriceTower.
57. Quoted in Arthur Lubow. "The Triumph of Frank Lloyd Wright." *Smithsonian*, August 2009. www.smithsonianmag.com/history-archaeology/The-Triumph-of-Frank-Lloyd-Wright.html?c=y&page=2.
58. Smith. *American Master: Frank Lloyd Wright*, p. 361.
59. Quoted in Westport Historical Society. "Hilla Rebay: A Baroness in Westport." www.westporthistory.org/exhibits/hilla-rebay-a-baroness-in-westport.
60. Quoted in Pfeiffer. *Frank Lloyd Wright, 1867–1959*, p. 81.
61. "*New York Times.* Frank Lloyd Wright Dies," April 10, 1959. www.nytimes.com/learning/general/onthisday/bday/0608.html.
62. Quoted in Pfeiffer, *The Essential Frank Lloyd Wright*, p. 438.

Chapter 6: The Light That Never Fails

63. Quoted in Jack Kolls. "The Legacy

and Triumphs of Frank Lloyd Wright." www.kolls.cscarolina.com/Home .html.

64. Kolls. "The Legacy and Triumphs of Frank Lloyd Wright."

65. Heinz. *Frank Lloyd Wright: Field Guide*, p. 449.

66. Quoted in Sommer. *Frank Lloyd Wright: American Architect for the Twentieth Century*, p. 6.

67. Sommer. *Frank Lloyd Wright: American Architect for the Twentieth Century*, p. 6.

68. Quoted in Tim Sandefur. "Frank Lloyd Wright's Humanism: Documentary on the Architect." http://findarticles.com/p/articles/mi_m1374/is_3_59/ai_54574817/pg_2.

69. Huxtable. *Frank Lloyd Wright*, pp. 203–204.

70. Lind. *Lost Wright*, p. 14.

71. Wright. *Frank Lloyd Wright: An Autobiography*, pp. 255–256.

72. Adkins. *Up Close*, p. 287.

73. Quoted in Pfeiffer. *Frank Lloyd Wright, 1867–1959*, p. 15.

For More Information

Books

Jan Adkins. *Up Close: Frank Lloyd Wright.* New York: Viking, 2007. A former art director for *National Geographic* and one-time college major in architecture, Adkins summarizes Wright's many contributions to architecture in this easy-to-read volume.

Trewin Copplestone. *Frank Lloyd Wright: A Retrospective View.* New York: Todtri, 2001. The author has put together an excellent collection of photos of Wright's buildings and supported them with an informative synopsis of his life and work.

Frances A. Davis. *Frank Lloyd Wright: Maverick Architect.* Minneapolis: Lerner, 1996. Written for high school–level readers, this well-researched and well-written volume will appeal to people of all ages.

Allan W. Green. *Building the Pauson House: The Letters of Frank Lloyd Wright and Rose Pauson.* San Francisco: Pomegranate, 2011. Green, a distant relative of Pauson's, presents a behind-the-scenes look at the activities, communications, and difficulties that typically accompanied the building of one of Wright's structures.

Thomas A. Heinz. *Frank Lloyd Wright: Field Guide.* Evanston, IL: Northwestern University Press, 2005. This volume lists and describes all of the more than five hundred buildings that Wright designed and built and is a must-read for Wright fans.

Edgar Kaufmann, ed. *Frank Lloyd Wright: An American Architecture.* San Francisco: Pomegranate, 2006. This easy-to-read book is a collection of fascinating and invaluable writings by Wright himself about the basic principles of architecture.

Edgar Kaufmann Jr. *Fallingwater: A Frank Lloyd Wright Country House.* New York: Abbeville, 2001. Kaufmann, son of the owners of Fallingwater and a close associate of Wright's during the house's construction, delivers one of the best of the many books about this architectural milestone.

Neil Levine. *The Architecture of Frank Lloyd Wright.* Princeton, NJ: Princeton University Press, 1996. This is widely viewed as the leading, most comprehensive modern study of Wright's work.

Carla Lind. *Lost Wright: Frank Lloyd Wright's Vanished Masterpieces.* New

York: Simon and Schuster, 1996. This fascinating book explores the 118 Wright buildings that were demolished over the years, telling when and how they were built and why they were torn down, all the while providing insights into both Wright and American society.

Haydn Middleton. *Frank Lloyd Wright.* Chicago: Heinemann Library, 2002. This brief but informative sysnopsis of Wright's life and work is aimed at junior high school students, but older people interested in Wright will benefit as well.

Bruce B. Pfeiffer. *Frank Lloyd Wright, 1867-1959: Building for Democracy.* Los Angeles: Taschen, 2006. A short but informative look at Wright's life and major works, featuring some rare photos of him at home with his family and visiting the work sites of some of his structures.

Bruce B. Pfeiffer, ed. *The Essential Frank Lloyd Wright: Critical Writings on Architecture.* Princeton, NJ: Princeton University Press, 2008. An excellent collection of first-person accounts by Wright, illuminating his long architectural career.

Meryle Secrest. *Frank Lloyd Wright.* New York: Knopf, 1992. This is still widely viewed as one of the best existing biographies of Wright.

Kathryn Smith. *Frank Lloyd Wright: American Master.* New York: Rizzoli, 2009. This book has one of the better

collections of high-quality photos of Wright's designs, along with a brief but well-written text about his career.

Robin L. Sommer. *Frank Lloyd Wright: American Architect for the Twentieth Century.* Greenwich, CT: Brompton, 1993. A noted art historian, Sommer summarizes in an easy-to-read format Wright's major accomplishments in architecture.

Websites

Animation of the Mile-High Skyscraper (www.youtube.com/watch?v=nR gICz41m_U). This excellent student animation brings to life Wright's mile-high building, the Illinois.

Art Institute of Chicago: Frank Lloyd Wright Collections (www.artic.edu/ aic/collections/artwork/artist/1009). Contains numerous examples of furniture, window dressings, and other furnishings that Wright designed for many of his houses.

Digital Archive of American Architecture: Frank Lloyd Wright (www .bc.edu/bc_org/avp/cas/fnart/fa267/ FLW.html). This site provides a list of links to articles and photos of some of Wright's most famous buildings.

Fallingwater (www.wright-house.com/ frank-lloyd-wright/fallingwater.html). Filled with helpful facts, this site has one of the best overviews on the Internet of Wright's most famous house.

Frank Lloyd Wright in Oak Park (http://oprf.com/Wright). A useful introduction to Wright's home and studio in Oak Park, the site has several links to tourist-related information.

The Johnson Wax Building (www .archiplanet.org/buildings/Johnson _Wax_Building.html). Part of the online Great Buildings series, this site contains several excellent photos of the interior of the JohnsonWax Building.

Keeping Faith with an Idea: A Time Line of the Guggenheim Museum, 1943–1959 (http://web.guggenheim .org/timeline/index.html). This factfilled site about the museum is part of one of its official celebrations.

The Legacy of Frank Lloyd Wright (www.pbs.org/flw/legacy/index.html). This is an introductory web page to filmmaker Ken Burns's retrospective of Wright and his achievements.

Index

Picture Credits

Cover: © H. Mark Weidman Photography/Alamy

© Alan Weintraub/Arcaid/Corbis, 36

© AP Images/Charles Rex Arbogast, 42 (bottom)

© AP Images/Morry Gash, 48

© Archive Images/Alamy, 18

© Bettmann/Corbis, 53, 55, 56, 61

© dk/Alamy, 82 (bottom)

© Farrell Grehan/Corbis, 71

© Field Museum Library/Getty Images, 25

© The Frank Lloyd Wright Foundation, AZ/Art Resource, NY, 15

© Frank Lloyd Wright Preservation Trust/Getty Images, 23

© G.E. Kidder Smith/Corbis, 42 (top), 74

© Hedrich Blessing Collection/Chicago History Museum/Getty Images, 31, 64

© H. Mark Weidman Photography/Alamy, 69

© Horace Bristol/Corbis, 58

© Hulton Archive/Getty Images, 20, 47

© Iain Masterton/Alamy, 97

© Joe Munroe/Hulton Archive/Getty Images, 9

© Joe Munroe/Photo Researchers, Inc., 89

© John Elk III/Alamy, 80

© Kenneth Johansson/Corbis, 66, 67

© Keystone View Company/FPG/Archive Photos/Getty Images, 95

© Lake County Museum/Getty Images, 50

© Lightworks Media/Alamy, 72-73

© LOOK Die Bildagentur der Fotografen GmbH/Alamy, 82 (top)

© Pat & Chuck Blackley/Alamy, 77

© Santi Visalli/Hulton Archive/Getty Images, 35

© Spencer Grant/Photo Researchers, Inc., 91

© Thomas A. Heinz/Corbis, 26

© Time & Life Pictures/Getty Images, 85

About the Author

Historian Don Nardo is best known for his books for young people about the ancient and medieval worlds. These include volumes on the arts of ancient cultures, including Mesopotamian arts and literature, Egyptian sculpture and monuments, Greek temples, Roman amphitheaters, medieval castles, and general histories of sculpture, painting, and architecture through the ages. Nardo lives with his wife, Christine, in Massachusetts.